The 5 Keys To Inner
PEACE

A STEP BY STEP PATH TO INNER PEACE AND PURPOSE

JOHN GEORGE

BALBOA.
PRESS

A DIVISION OF HAY HOUSE

Balboa Press books may be ordered through booksellers or by contacting:

Balboa Press
A Division of Hay House
1663 Liberty Drive
Bloomington, IN 47403
www.balboapress.com.au
1 (877) 407-4847

ISBN: 978-1-5043-0011-7 (sc)
ISBN: 978-1-5043-0012-4 (e)

Print information available on the last page.

Balboa Press rev. date: 12/04/2015

~ *Acknowledgements* ~

I would like to thank all my teachers and mentors throughout my life. In particular, thank you to my first counsellor, Geraldine Burton, who helped me through my darkest time.

I would also like to acknowledge my teachers of wisdom including Eckhart Tolle, Dr John Demartini, Dr Wayne Dyer and all the authors of books who point towards that place of peace.

I would especially like to thank all of the people who I have coached because it was your commitment to the process which convinced me that this was a science to inner peace.

I now feel grateful for my years spent in depression because this period of my life was where my greatest lessons were learned. It was only when I hit rock bottom did I look to reach out for help and begin my life-long journey of learning and expanding my awareness.

I dedicate this book to anyone who feels they have reached a point of no return. I was once in that dark place too. I feel blessed to be able to share what I have learned during my journey towards a place of peace which is beyond definition.

Contents

~ Prologue ~

*Someone I loved once gave me a box full of darkness. It took me years
to understand that this too, was a gift. ~ Mary Oliver*

It's back in the year 2000. I'm driving in my white Holden Commodore. It's raining hard and I've cranked the windshield wipers up as fast as they'll go. My eyes are filled with tears.

That was the night I decided I couldn't go on with life; I'd given up.

As I was driving, I kept thinking, *How can I make this look like an accident so that people don't know I purposefully killed myself?*

I thought about driving off a cliff and making it looks like I lost control but when I fast-forwarded to my funeral and seeing my mother heartbroken, I couldn't go through with it.

It was the night I also realised that I had to swallow my pride. Up until that day, I had been someone who seemed to always think that he could solve everything himself. I didn't realise at the time that the problem was my mind and that I wasn't in control of it.

So I made the decision that night: perhaps I didn't know everything and that I should and would seek assistance.

A close friend of mine suggested a psychologist whom she had seen and highly recommended. At this point, I had nothing to lose so I decided to make the phone call.

Within six months, I was completely transformed and had come out of my depression. Things had become a lot clearer and I started to realise that I wanted to become a teacher.

After twelve months, I finished the counselling. However, I was left with a feeling that there was still so much more to life. I wanted to feel truly happy and completely at peace and I wanted to know exactly what it would take to get there.

So for the next thirteen years, I went on a special journey. I researched, I read books, I attended seminars and workshops but it wasn't until about five years ago that a permanent shift happened.

My family noticed and said to me, "John, you've changed! You are so much calmer these days. You don't seem to react to things the way you used to. How did you do it? Can you teach us?"

At first, I wasn't really sure what exactly had happened so it was difficult to explain, let alone share my 'secret'.

At the time leading up to this transformation, I had been listening, repeatedly, to the audio book *A New Earth* by Eckhart Tolle in my car.

Now while I admit that this had a role in influencing how I felt about my life and myself to bring about the transformation in me, I knew that there was more to it. I decided I had to take a step back to observe what had happened and to take a look at the bigger picture.

One of my life mentors explained in a seminar how humans have ultimate strategies for most things in life such as finding the right partner: to learn to love yourself first, and succeeding in business: to focus on servicing and helping others. However, there isn't yet any ultimate strategy for finding and maintaining inner peace.

It was then that something inside me said, *Well, you've found inner peace and experienced it for yourself so there must be some special sequence of events that occurred or is occurring on a daily basis for you to feel this way.*

This became the second reason that set me out on my mission to determine how I had discovered inner peace.

As I went on this reflective journey, I realised that there were a few things I had originally thought that might bring me inner peace.

I had looked at money but then I noticed some wealthy people were still out there killing themselves from a lack of fulfilment in their lives. I looked at work and career as well but I noticed that while some people may manage to secure a job they like, the rest of their lives still is a disaster.

Then there are some people who spent years and thousands of dollars on education, pursuing a career they thought they would like only to find a few years later that they have stopped enjoying it and no longer find fulfilment in it. So I crossed that one off too.

I also thought that perhaps it comes down to finding your soul mate and the 'happily ever after'. However, I can tell you now that it didn't seem to matter who my partner was, I still had never found myself completely at peace with my life. You may know of people who have wonderful partners but are still not at peace; they still seem to be missing something.

Once I ruled out those three things, I asked the most important question of myself, "*When DON'T I feel at peace?*"

I noticed everything that knocked me off balance fell into five categories which became the five keys to inner peace. I realised that I had balanced all five simultaneously for me to feel at peace.

After coaching adults and teenagers on the simple science, I got a gentle tap from several people suggesting I write a book so I could help more people who were ready to apply the simple action steps.

My life has gone on an amazing journey: from depression to not knowing what I wanted to do with my life, to becoming a teacher, a motivational speaker and a life coach.

Everything in my teachings has come out of that dark place I once found myself in. I now know that it all happened for a reason so I have no regrets or resentment whatsoever against myself or anyone else.

In this book, I'm going to outline a step-by-step system of action steps that will help you find balance and inner peace if you commit to taking the actions.

The fact that you are reading this book means you have reached a point in your life where you've decided you want balance and an end to drama.

This book will show you exactly how to achieve that. It won't involve actions that get you way out of your comfort zone. It is, in fact, quite simple.

The universe was created from silence, from a place of calm. Everything came from that void, that invisible field of energy. By tapping into your own inner peace, you will be entering that state of calm where all true creativity and abundance originates.

Therefore, rather than striving to make things happen and struggling through life, you must first realise that you won't find peace by having enough money or the right job or chasing achievements. It's the other way around. You must find peace first and then everything else will flow to you.

Every area of your life will start to improve and you will only see abundance in your life because you won't feel a lack or shortage of anything.

As I outline the Five Keys to Inner Peace, I'm going to describe for you some very simple strategies to achieving the most fulfilment in all areas of your life.

You will get to the point where you are able to realise that you are already amazing, you are divine and that you can truly create endlessly from that special place of peace.

So my question to you is, "What have you got to lose?"

Enjoy your journey towards inner peace and the abundance that flows naturally from it.

~ Introduction ~

WHY INNER PEACE IS ESSENTIAL TO HAVING AN ABUNDANT LIFE?

Abundance is your state of being. ~ Sargam Mishra

I have met many people, over the years, who have a yearning to manifest and be productive with their lives and to experience great profits in the meantime.

With many of the people I have coached, when I ask them my first question, "What is the one thing you would love to have as a result of the coaching?" Many will reply, "I want to manifest and be abundant." For some others, "I just want to find my purpose in life."

No matter what they told me, I knew I had to teach them inner peace because I felt that I had stumbled onto a universal blueprint for manifesting effortlessly or what many people would call 'Flow' or being 'in the zone'.

I will have to rewind seven or eight years to describe how I came to the realisation of this universal law.

Eight years ago, I was a full-time teacher and it was an unwritten expectation that for the school to be productive and profitable, we needed to be getting results to make the school an attractive place for parents to enrol their children. The logical solution for me was to focus on the performance of the students, particularly in exams.

It was here that I began to teach students simple ways to get organised, study smarter strategies for learning more in less time and an exam game plan for zero stress which would allow them to perform when it mattered most: in exams.

All of the system is outlined in my book *Teenage Zen* and I thought all of those strategies would be enough to have every student I taught improving their results.

However, it didn't take me long to see that some students were improving and others were not. I soon realised that there was a prerequisite to performing well: purpose, because students wouldn't study unless they had a strong reason or motivation to do so. Consequently, this became my focus.

I knew I had to motivate or inspire young people to want to do the weekly study if I was going to get more students to improve their results.

I researched into motivation and trialled various techniques. I developed a two-minute process for motivating any child to study. (You can download the free eBook, which explains the technique at www.infloweducation.com.au)

I was confident all my students would improve their results from here yet again, many students had indeed improved but not all of them. I soon realised there was a prerequisite to purpose: inner peace.

The students who had their 'buttons' easily pushed or were not confident enough in themselves didn't seem to have the energy or focus to study regularly.

When young people are looking for ways to feel better about life, they don't tend to think of study. After some soul-searching in my own life, the Five Keys to Inner Peace was born.

Now I had students performing at their best without struggling and straining. They still had their social life and some even worked part-time.

It wasn't until the past year that I realised it is a universal blueprint: Peace comes first, purpose then becomes clear, leading to high performance results in productivity and profits.

A quote from one of the greatest minds of the twentieth century, Albert Einstein, had me baffled for years, "I want to know the mind of God, the rest is details."

That was until earlier this year when I had several people close to me, including my speaking agent and consultant, suggesting I teach businesses.

I looked around for examples of people who are high performers and productive, who seemed to be operating from a place of flow. Warren Buffet, Oprah and Roger Federer were some that came to mind. However, I had overlooked the greatest producer we know: life itself.

I suddenly saw the planets, stars and other heavenly bodies as the productivity and the profits.

I saw the high performance and the willingness to continually evolve, not just creating but running live updates to adapt to what was required. Why would the universe go to all that trouble for billions of years unless it had a strong purpose?

It became clear to me that the purpose was to create a playground, a way for invisible energy to know itself through form. The universe is here to serve, asking for nothing in return.

Where did the universe originate? It started with silence: inner peace. In space, there is no sound. There was the clear order again. Peace came first before purpose, which leads to high performance and productivity and profits.

The blueprint is there in nature. Observe a mango tree for example: It produces mangoes which can be sold for profits. It performs if it is planted in the right environment. Why does it go to the trouble of growing from a tiny seed into a large mango tree? Its purpose is to serve life with its fruit for any living creature in need of food. Where did the tree start from? As a tiny seed in the ground where there is no sound: inner peace.

The Five Keys to Inner Peace is a simple science, which will allow purpose and vision to become crystal clear. From there, you will naturally be a high performer, which will lead to productivity and profit.

Most importantly, you will be able to 'hold the space' for people to feel that they can just be themselves in your company.

Take time to observe the universal blueprint of peace, purpose and performance in universal creation, in nature on earth and in high performers who operate from a place of Flow.

It's time to sow the seeds.

~ Chapter One ~
WHAT IS INNER PEACE?

Inner peace begins the moment you choose not to allow another
person or event control your emotions. ~ Ra Ramsey

When I found inner peace, the first question I got asked was, "What exactly is inner peace? I don't understand it!" My answer was always this, "It's pretty hard to define inner peace because it's not any thing on its own."

Similarly when I ask people "What is silence?" They generally reply that silence is simply the removal or the absence of sound.

The same goes for "What is space?" Space is not a thing in itself. It is merely the absence of any object; the absence of matter.

So the best way I can describe inner peace is the removal of the drama you create in your life with your own mind.

However, before I discuss what inner peace is, let me explain the importance of it. The reason why inner peace is so crucial is because anything beautiful, useful or productive in the universe has been created from a calm, peaceful place.

This means that if you want to create anything of value in your life, something of real beauty that means a lot to you, then it's essential to find that place, to be in the state of inner peace.

Without balance and inner peace, life takes us on an endless emotional rollercoaster. We hit massive highs and lows. At some point, if you are like me, you have probably grown quite tired of riding on that rollercoaster and being constantly at the mercy of your emotions.

What you most likely want is simply a calm and balanced state of being, in which you don't fluctuate too much mentally or emotionally—where the gap between your worst days and your best days, the highs and the lows, starts to shrink.

Until you reach that balanced state, you are always going to feel like something is missing. When you find that balance in your life and have inner peace, you will be able to create whatever it is that you want in your life.

You will have the ability to create the abundance you want, have a business that you are proud of, make the money that you need, be able to be an awesome role model for your children and so on.

Many people make the mistake of thinking that they're going to find inner peace by chasing something out there. You know how it goes, *If I get the right job, or I find the perfect partner, or I have enough money...* But I'm here to tell you that it actually happens the other way around.

Once you have inner peace and your purpose becomes clear, you will realise that all these other things will come surprisingly easily and you won't feel like you are struggling anymore.

When I felt inner peace for myself and experienced that permanent shift, how did things change for me? I was still a teacher but how I was teaching changed forever.

I developed specific strategies and a simple method, which I incorporated into my teaching. Essentially, I removed all the excuses that children have for not doing well at school.

From there, my tutoring business grew and I began receiving requests from adults to coach them as well. That was when I decided to expand my business by becoming a motivational speaker in high schools and a life coach for adults.

Initially, I would speak and informally tutor in my role as a casual teacher, trying to motivate children and teenagers, then I realised I heard this a lot, "Have you thought of being a motivational speaker because that was really good!" And since I kept hearing this, I realised that the universe was giving me signs and pointing me in a certain direction.

This is what happens when you find that place of peace. The same thing happened with the start of my tutoring business about eight years ago.

I was teaching full-time in a high school and towards the end of the year, the boys in my class began asking me, "Are we going to have you next year? I really hope you're our Maths teacher next year." My reply was always, "We don't get to choose who we teach. We're just told at the start of the year, 'Here you go, these are your classes.'"

However, because I kept hearing these remarks over and over again, I realised that they were signs pushing me to start a tutoring business and that was how it eventuated.

Further down the track, about four years ago, I kept hearing, "You should write a book! All this stuff you are teaching about—how to get motivated and how to study—you should write a book on it", and like before, I realised that I was being guided.

So I finally put it all together in a book for teenagers and their parents, called *Teenager Zen: A Simple Path to Academic Success and Inner Peace.*

My point here is that it's mandatory to get to that place of peace because once you are there, you no longer need to struggle. Others may take notice of you and suggest how you can utilise your gifts and talents.

Since you won't be caught up in your mind anymore, you will be able to hear these people and notice the signs guiding you in a certain direction.

There will be no more drama; the noise and buzz will have stopped and because of that, it will become very clear what it is you should do with your life and how you can best serve people on this planet.

You can stop chasing money, the perfect career or the perfect relationship. Once you find that place of inner peace, all those areas of your life will naturally flourish.

You will be able to see and think more clearly and be better able to make decisions that positively affect you and those around you.

The source of abundance is inner peace. Abundance doesn't come from chasing things; it comes from allowing and the best way to allow, is to know that you already have it and that all you need to do is be in a state of peace and gratitude to unlock your full potential.

In the animated family film, *Kung Fu Panda 2*, there is a scene where the Dojo Master, Shifu, explains to his apprentice, Po, what inner peace is. Po was really impressed by how calm Master Shifu was and how things always seemed to be happening very easily for him so he wanted to know how he did it. The Master's reply was simply, "Inner peace". He explained how some people find inner peace through meditating in a cave for fifty years without food or water while others find it through suffering.

Now while my own journey evolved from a place of suffering, what I outline in the Five Keys to Inner Peace involves no suffering whatsoever; only very simple action steps.

If you take these action steps just as I have outlined them, you will find that your whole world will change.

Gone will be the turbulence of the massive highs and lows. A calm, centred human being who knows exactly what they need to do and allows life to live through them will replace all that.

If you take the action steps in every part of your life, you are going to feel calmer; you are going to feel a sense of purpose in your life.

You are going to feel like you can be an expert because you will have the energy and clarity to research into what it is that you really love. And from there, work opportunities will flow to you in abundance.

There will be promotions coming to you at work because you are operating from a place of peace and calm.

There will be opportunities for starting your own business or joint ventures with other people. And since you are operating from a place of peace in your work and opportunities are coming, the money will be flowing.

From there, you will soon be able to have the house, the car, the lifestyle and the travel that you want and be able to donate more money to others and most importantly, provide an awesome life for your family.

You will also be a great role model for your children. All this will just naturally flow from that place of calm. People will shake their head in disbelief at the transformation in you and they will start to ask themselves, *If they can do it, why can't I?*

You will be creating a new legacy for your children or family and friends who will then have a template for how to be at peace; they will have a living example: You.

No longer will you need to lecture them repeatedly because you will be the walking, breathing example of what it's like to be at peace and you will be able to pass this on to your family.

You will be breaking the cycle of drama in your own family and your future grandchildren and great grandchildren will be thankful that you took these steps and that you had the courage to break the cycle.

Once you find that place of inner peace, you are also going to inspire your friends and co-workers and will empower them in the same manner.

When I tutor or coach, it's nothing I say to people that really causes the transformation in them. It's the *doing*.

It's by being an example myself and taking the initiative to step out and lead the way that I have been able to inspire the people I coach, as well as my family and friends, to take similar actions.

The same will apply for you. You will be a living example and an inspiration to all those around you by taking the actions yourself.

Finally, from that place of inner peace, you are going to value yourself so much more. You will be more conscious of what you put into your body. You will have the energy to exercise and be more productive in your day. You will begin to look and feel younger than you have in a long time.

The reason I called my business InFlow Education is because I have learned that it is always from that place of inner peace that everything flows naturally.

When you get into the flow of life, you start to realise that life is not a struggle, but rather a place with a current that you can tap into and simply flow along with. You can control the oars and guide where you are going but you don't need to paddle upstream, to struggle and work so hard you miss out on the simple joys of life.

Once you find inner peace, you are going to find that everything will just flow naturally to you and you will be able to create the life for yourself that you have always dreamed of.

Taking Action

Watch *Kung Fu Panda 2*, which is a great movie for teaching about inner peace, what it is and how to recognise it. Additionally, it's a great laugh with a great moral and is perfect for kicking back with the kids for a couple of hours.

Read a variety of books on the topic of inner peace. I don't want what I talk about to be your only source of information. Though you do not need to be an expert on the subject, I recommend you expose yourself to other principles taught by other people with their own experiences, to help you develop a well-rounded view on what it means to be at peace and the importance of it.

The more that you can read and research on any particular topic from various authors, the more you can find your common thread for what feels just right for you. You don't need to believe everything you learn; just take what you like and what you feel you can use and throw out what you don't need.

In my own journey of learning and discovery, I've always taken what feels right for me and then distilled that knowledge into the simplest path I know. You will find that the information in this book is really as simple as I can make it.

I don't want to overload you with technical information or weigh you down with too many new thoughts and ideas. I have focussed on making it all about the actions and how you can attain inner peace in the simplest and easiest way possible.

I was able to do it myself without anybody guiding me directly. You can do it also. Anybody can do it. It simply starts with the conscious decision to begin taking the actions.

## Chapter Two

THE MAJOR ROADBLOCK TO INNER PEACE: THE EGO

When you allow your ego to control your thoughts, everything
you believe becomes an illusion. ~ Rusty Eric

As I mentioned in the definition, inner peace is the removal of drama. The major obstacle to inner peace is your ego. It is important to have a clear understanding as to what your ego is, otherwise you will constantly be confused as to who you really are, *Is this me? Or is this something a part of me?*

Getting crystal clear about your ego is going to allow you to find out exactly who you are by helping you to realise who you are not.

Often, people come to me and say, "I just want to know who I am. I'm trying to figure it out but I have no idea." I tell them that rather than trying to figure out who they are, if they get clear about who they are not by the simple process of elimination, they will be much closer to discovering the answer.

Dr Wayne Dyer gives an excellent explanation of the ego by using the acronym EGO - **E**dging **G**od **O**ut. This is all about moving away from your God-like nature and gravitating or moving towards the animal nature in you because your ego is the animal part of your brain that is all about survival. It just wants to keep you alive at all costs; that will always drive everything it does.

Rather than giving you dictionary definitions, I am going to give you some examples of the ego at work.

You may recall when you were four or five years old and you were playing with a toy or you might have kids of your own now and sometimes notice this: They play with a toy and then after a while, they get bored of it so they put the toy away in the toy box and they don't look at it for some time. Along comes another kid who wants to play with this toy, which all of a sudden, becomes the first child's favourite toy once again, "Hey, don't touch that toy! That's my favourite! I love that toy!" This is the ego in the first child through the form of possessiveness.

The ego also pops up when you are playing sports, board games or engage in any competitive activity. It's the part of you that, when you win, shouts inside: *Yeah, I'm better than other people! I'm better than you!* And alternatively, when you lose, you are just shattered because your ego is the part of you that always says, *I'm better,* or, *I'm worse,* and constantly compares you to others on a vertical hierarchy. The ego loves to pop up in a competitive environment.

When I was growing up, I was obsessed with playing sports. There wasn't a sport I wouldn't try and I wanted to be perfect at them all. When I look back now, I realise that a major factor for that was my ego's need to feel better than other people and so it just wasn't good enough for me to be okay at sports; I had to be perfect at it and that was partly why I didn't do so well in my academic school life the first time around.

I was so focussed on sports because it gave me a temporary sense of satisfaction. It was an area in which I could be better at some things than other people and it made my ego feel good.

For those of you who are shy in certain situations, I can tell you now that your shyness is purely the work of the ego—the five-year-old inside you that says: *Shh, don't say anything. You might look worse than what you already are. If you mess up, you could make a fool of yourself.*

Once you become aware of that, you realise that you don't need to be shy because shyness comes from valuing other people's opinions over your own.

Once you remove that and you are aware of the ego's need to not look bad in other people's eyes, you will be free to live your life however you choose.

You will also begin to realise that you don't wish to spend time with every person that you meet, so why would you expect everyone you meet to want to hang out with you?

Once you look at it from this point of view, you start to realise the one thing that is holding you back is simply the ego's need; it's just the five-year-old in you that you can calm down at any time.

The ego is also the part of you that always has to be right. You might know someone who swears it's white when it's black. It's that five-year-old ego in them saying: *I need to be right because if I'm wrong, then you're right which means that you're better than me.* It argues to the point where it believes it just can't be wrong, even if it really is.

I was once a prime example of this. I feel really sorry for my sister, Amelia, who's three years my junior. When we were younger, I always had to have the last word. I could never be wrong. I had to argue and argue until I was 'right'.

Fortunately since then, I've been able to transform that need to be right into an area of my life that inspires me. So whilst I still have the need to be right, I have shifted it to serve me in a higher purpose. The need to be right is now what drives me to research, attend workshops and seminars and read books.

I need to be right about how to be at peace and how to help others live an inspired life; I need to know the best ways to achieve this so that I can help as many people as possible.

You see, I don't need to feel shame around the need to be right. I simply had to channel it in such a way that it serves me so that my ego now realises that I can be right without telling other people they are wrong.

The ego is also the part of you that wants you to conform and have a herd mentality. As I mentioned earlier, the ego is the animal part of your brain.

You have probably noticed that in the animal world, animals tend to flock together in groups because, instinctively, they know that if they stay together, their chances of survival increase. If one were to stand out from the mob and walk its own path, it would be more vulnerable and more susceptible to being attacked. However, we are not simply animals. We were created as higher beings with the ability to reason and think for ourselves rather than blindly follow instincts; we were built for a higher purpose. Thus, for you to live an inspired life and to be uniquely you, you will need to overcome and be aware of the part of your brain that says: *Just follow the crowd. Just keep your head down. Just take whatever you can get. Don't be different because if you're different, people might attack you but if you're just like everybody else then nobody will notice you and you'll be able to stay alive longer.* Listening to the ego whenever it pops up and whispers this is ultimately what's going to hold you back in life and keeps you from achieving your dreams or accomplishing what you were made to accomplish.

The ego has been described as 'the voice in your head'. If you are wondering, *What voice in my head?* That's the one—you just found it. It's critical to understand that your ego is not your enemy. It's just the five-year-old inside you that you need to win over and be conscious of so you can get it to serve you. Many people, without realising it, are letting their five-year-old ego drive while they sit in the passenger seat. Every now and then, they wake up and think, *How did I get here? What was I thinking doing that? What was I thinking going out with X?*

So the bad news is that the ego is with you for life. There is no getting rid of your ego. The good news is that you can switch places. You can take over as the driver while putting the ego back in the passenger seat where it belongs. You can be aware of the ego and understand its need to feel safe and secure.

Once your ego sees, *There's a lot in this for me,* by you taking a new path of peace and abundance and serving the planet, it will be on board. It's not going to fight you. It's going to actually want you to do as you desire but you've got to convince it. Remember, it's a five-year-old; it needs explaining and it needs constant reminders that the action steps you are going to take are actually just going to give it more of what it loves.

When you become aware of your ego, you create separation, a bit of space between who you are and who you are not. Your ego is your thinking mind, which is a tool that you can use. However, most people fall into the trap of believing their mind is who they are, leading them to be confused about who they actually are. Your egoic mind is just a tool that you can put down and stop using at any time. I'm going to teach you how to do that and how to create the space between who you are and who you are not so that you don't get confused; then you will be able to start getting closer to figuring out who you really are and what your purpose is in life.

To notice the ego in your own mind, you must start to become an observer. If you went up to a child and said, "You're stinky!" or otherwise did something to offend them, they would be hurt and most likely react by becoming defensive or firing back to protect themselves. Next time you find yourself on the receiving end of an offensive remark, stop and examine yourself to see if you are reacting to the situation immaturely, much like a five-year-old would and once you realise that it is just your ego reacting immaturely, observe it and allow it to pass. Just watch it and understand that your natural, immediate reaction might be to defend, to get angry and to let this person's opinions generally get the better of you. Take a couple of breaths and simply observe, both of yourself and the other person. Doing so will give you a greater awareness of what the ego is and how it affects you. You will become more familiar with the five-year-old inside you and thus, be able to control it better.

The thing about the ego is it always wants more; it's never satisfied; it can never have enough. If you put food in front of a wild animal, often, it would keep eating until there was no more food, regardless of its hunger. This is because it doesn't know for certain whether the food would keep coming or if there is even going to be any more at a later stage. Therefore, it would eat and eat as much as it could just in case there was no more food later. Likewise, the ego never knows when enough is enough—when it has had enough sex, material possessions, food, money or power—it will never stop wanting more and it will eventually drag you into the ground as you go on an endless journey attempting to fulfil these unquenchable desires.

There are some songs that highlight the ego beautifully, such as The Rolling Stones' *I Can't Get No Satisfaction* whilst Eminem's *Monster* is all about the voice in your head and the constant struggle to make peace with it. It is this struggle that drives you. You need to make peace with it rather than try to defeat it. Also, if you listen to the song and watch the music video for pop star, Katy Perry's *Dark Horse*, you will see that it's all about the ego and the two sides in you—your god-like or light side and your ego or shadow side. The song *Demons* by Imagine Dragons is all about being aware of the 'dark side' of yourself. You can listen to these songs, when you get a chance, to become more familiar with the nature of the ego. Also listen to the lyrics in other songs you hear and identify the ones that make mention of the ego in their own way. This can be a simple way to practise awareness and observe the ego and its effect on people. By taking a look at pop culture and Hollywood, you will always find numerous examples of many people, both fictional and real, who either chose to let their ego drive or have learned how to put the ego to sleep in the passenger seat while they take charge of their own life.

I have tried to make the concept of the ego as simple as possible for you here. However, if you want to delve even deeper into the subject, read Eckhart Tolle's *A New Earth*. In this book, he provides extensive explanation of what the ego is and how exactly it affects us as human beings. Additionally, check out works by Dr Wayne Dyer.

I also recommend watching the film, *Peaceful Warrior*, which outlines and shines light on the ego. It is based on the book, *The Way of the Peaceful Warrior* by Dan Millman. I have watched it several times and learned so much every time.

Hopefully by now you have a greater understanding of what your ego is and the roles it plays in your life. From here on, you will realise that you are not your ego and it is simply a side of you that you can control. Once you know who you are not, you will be able to take the first step towards figuring out who you are, which is all part of the process to experiencing inner peace.

Once you start to become aware of the ego, you become somebody who is proactive rather than reactive. You will stop riding an emotional rollercoaster and you will banish the victim mentality. You will start to realise, *I really am a master of my destiny, not a victim of my history.* You will also feel a great sense of relief and peace to realise who you are not, which will bring you much closer to who you really are.

Taking Action

Begin to make a conscious effort to stop and observe the ego at work in your interactions with people and in other people's interactions. Simply notice it and be aware of it. You can also start to journal or take notes of the times when your ego wants to raise its head and defend you by attacking others. Start to create more space around it when you notice this. Take a few deep breaths. Calm your mind.

Do some reading to learn more about the ego and the roles it plays in your life. Read *A New Earth* by Eckhart Tolle. Read books by Dr Wayne Dyer and Dr John Demartini. Do your own research into what the ego is all about to get a clearer picture of it in your mind.

Schedule time to watch the film *Peaceful Warrior* several times. You will learn more with each time you watch it.

~ *Chapter Three* ~

THE FIVE KEYS AND THE SEVEN AREAS OF LIFE

To live is the rarest thing in the world. Most people just exist. ~ Oscar Wilde

Some of the people I've coached applied the Five Keys over a period of five to six weeks. Some have done it over ten to twelve weeks by integrating the application of a new key into their routine every two weeks or so. I recommend you go through them over the course of ten to twelve weeks to give yourself time, to fully apply the actions and let the system integrate into your biology.

I've seen clients transformed time and time again before my eyes in as little as four or five sessions. When I first outlined the Five Keys system and began coaching it to my clients, my ego was saying: *Make sure the coaching goes on for at least twelve months or even two years so that you can make enough money from them.* However, my spirit said: *Why? There's no need for that if you can get them there sooner. More people will come anyway. The money will come. You don't need to worry about that.*

I was determined not only to find and break down the science behind inner peace but also to be able to share it with others and offer the simplest and fastest way to help them achieve it.

Before moving on, we are going to look at how inner peace affects all seven areas of your life, which I will be referring to in this book as: *Spiritual, Intellectual, Work, Money, Family, Friends* and *Health.* I will be outlining some of the many benefits that will come to each of these areas of your life once you have reached a state of peace and balance.

Firstly, let's take a look at Spiritual. When you apply the action of the Five Keys in your life and begin to experience inner peace, you will begin to know God. You will have a spiritual connection to the Source of Life. You will realise that you have always been guided throughout your life and that you have never been punished or a victim. The universe was really just trying to wake you up, to get your attention, for you to learn things, to meet new people, to have experiences you needed that lead you to this path of spiritual growth. Not to mention, you will possess a great sense of peace and calm—a balanced state of being, which is ultimately where all important decisions and creative ideas come from. You will begin to have the clarity you need to make important choices and find inspiration that will help you unlock your full potential.

From inner peace, you might discover you have the energy and the desire to search for truth in all religions and in all other spiritual teachings, so that you can gain a greater glimpse into the perfection of life and the spiritual connection between humans and the Creator. While I was raised as a Catholic, once I found inner peace, I wanted to read text from all religions because I wanted to find the common truth. My shift to inner peace allowed for this personal quest of spiritual growth and discovery to happen.

When I'm asked, "Do you believe in God?" I answer, "I know God. I see God in the tree that came from one tiny seed. I see God in the animals. I see God in humans. I see God in everything that's around me."

My experiences of balancing out and finding the perfection to every event are further evidence of God. Once you have inner peace, you will know God for yourself. You will have a direct experience. It will no longer be something you simply believe in that requires great amounts of faith. You will realise that there is proof to the unity of the *uni*-verse.

Whenever I look back at the winding journey of my life, I know that everything had a reason and a purpose. How could there be no God with such divine order in the seeming chaos? I'm not suggesting once you have found inner peace that you will need to leave your religion. What I simply mean is that you may find you are inspired to search for truth in other sources. Through this, you may find that you have a greater connection to your own religion or it may means that you don't want to follow any one particular religion. Regardless, you will feel a strong, spiritual connection to the Life Giver. Just as the branches of a tree cannot bear life of their own without being connected to the tree itself, you will realise that without a connection to the source of all life, a life of true abundance can never fully flourish.

Next, let's take a look at the Intellectual area of your life. Once you have inner peace, you are going to find that you can think more clearly and that your energy is flowing since there is no more clutter in your mind. For this reason, you will have the energy to research into what it is that you really want to learn about. You can become an expert. You will start to devour information and have a thirst for new knowledge and insight. You will find the motivation to learn more and more about things that you are passionate about and that are highest on your values.

As a high school student, I didn't do a lot of reading. I was not particularly fond of it. I had a difficult time focussing in class. I wasn't engaged. I wasn't motivated. However, when the shift to inner peace happened, I began to read more than I ever had before. I also started listening to audio books and found that they are an excellent way to engage myself in learning while my hands were full or my eyes were tired. Over the years, I have invested time in seeking and devouring knowledge, gathering insight on my topics of interest from many sources. I have become, what can be considered, an expert in my field. I learn as much as I can about human potential and how to get the most out of people. My desire to help others and to share my knowledge has lead me to read certain books, attend workshops and seminars to give me greater awareness on the best methods for reaching out and teaching people. You will also find that once you have reached a state of balance and inner peace, your desire for growth and enhancing your knowledge will motivate you to learn more than ever before. This will enable you to pass on your knowledge and experience to others to truly make a difference.

The next area of your life is Work or your vocation. Most people make the mistake of thinking that they will find peace once they find their calling—what it is they should do for a living. I disagree! Once you find peace, you will discover your calling and when it comes, that calling will be loud and clear. You will be getting messages and signs from all over the place and you will realise what you are meant to be doing. It may not means that you need to change your current job or career. It may simply means *how* you perform your current job changes, so you come back a different person, focussed on providing service for others and realising that you can make a difference in your current capacity. As a result, you will start to become a leader in your workplace. You will get noticed and promotions will come to you. You may be asked to train or mentor colleagues in how to be at peace as well so that the atmosphere in the workplace is calm and hence, more productive. It may be that you decide to run your own business from that place of calm. The point is you will just know what to do. The actions you must take will be clear. The right people will come along at the right time. You will start to see that the key to true happiness and fulfilment is to focus on serving others.

When I'm working with adults or teenagers and they are confused about what they want to do with their life, I just get them to ask themselves these questions: *What is the greatest service I can give to humanity? What is the greatest way I can help others? Is it through a service or perhaps by means of a product?*

Once they realise that they can do anything they love and how they can help others through that work, the confusion and doubt disappear; the clarity and confidence soar.

Really, there are only two things that will cloud your judgement when it comes to what you should do with your secondary purpose in life—what you should do with your life in terms of career. Those two things are fear concerning money and other people's opinions.

You need to understand that the ego is the animal part of your brain and it says: *If you don't earn enough money, you won't be able to buy food. If you don't have food, you will die!* When people stay in the animal mode, the unconscious mode in which the ego has the driver's seat, they take whatever they can get to ensure their survival whilst abandoning their dreams. The idea of taking risks or stepping out of their ego's comfort zone holds them back. They would never learn to live life to the fullest nor would they ever reach their full potential.

The second reason carries even more weight for many. Most people don't do what they really want because they let other people's opinions hold them back. However, if you take the time to observe life around you, you would realise that the people who tell you that you can't do something are generally the ones who haven't had the courage to follow their own dreams. So to see somebody else, including their own child, fulfilling their dreams in life can be quite confronting.

Realise that the only person who knows what you should be doing with your life is you. Otherwise, it's a bit like asking people for directions to your house when you're the only one who knows where your house is and what it looks like.

If you look at every industry on the planet, there isn't one industry in which somebody somewhere hasn't made a lot of money. Look at garbage collection. The people who run the waste management companies make a lot of money. If you could come up with a better way to get rid of waste, you would be a billionaire.

I have met people who were doing well financially as bakers, solicitors, carpenters and so on. The point is it's not about the *what*; it's the *how* that makes you successful and able to make a difference in the world. The common thread with all these people I have met is that they are doing what they love and they truly find the enjoyment in what they are doing. They do their work with a purpose and they do it wholeheartedly. They value themselves because they know they are a valuable part of the economy.

One needs not be a multimillionaire to be happy but if you wake up every day knowing you are being of service to humanity and nobody has to twist your arm to get out of bed, then you know you've found your calling. The more you become an expert in your chosen field of work, the more opportunities will come to you. You will find that you will meet the right people. Your business will grow. You may become a mentor, a consultant or a manager. You may choose to write books or a column on the type of work you do to help inspire others. Opportunities that you never thought possible will open up.

My motivational speaking and the writing of my first book, both came as surprises to me. However, because I took the risks necessary to make them happen, things naturally evolved from there.

The same will happen for you when you are making all your major decisions from a calm place and not having to blindly guess whether you are doing the 'right thing'. When you are making better business and financial decisions, you will be saving more money, spending less on things you don't need and will even be able to share your resources with others or provide jobs for people through your innovation in your industry.

The thing I have learned in life is that there are really only two root emotions: love and fear. All other secondary emotions come from these. When you practise inner peace, you are tapping into love, to God, to the abundance that's all around you. When you let the ego control you, you are in the fear mode. But once you have inner peace, the answer to the question "What is my purpose in life?" becomes very clear. The fear disappears, you will start to realise that only you can decide what to do with your life and that the *how* is more important than the *what*. You will realise that if you begin to focus more on service for others that your career will flourish. You won't need to worry about work; you will have plenty of work at your job or in your business. The business will flow to you with a considerable less amount of struggling and striving on your part. What you do with your life in regards to career may change several times throughout your life, but the motivation and inspiration in how you perform will remain the same.

Inner peace will also help you create a natural abundance and harmonious flow in your money life. When you have peace, you will no longer be chasing money. When you are genuinely focussing on a serving others, you will find that the money will just be attracted to you. So rather than you chasing money, the money will seem to follow you. The opportunities will come flooding in.

If you went outside and tried to chase butterflies with a net, it would be difficult at best. Not only would you exhaust yourself, your work would be futile as the butterflies would continue to fly out of reach, successfully escaping your desperate attempts. You might catch one or two at most. This is how it can be with money; sometimes the more you chase it, the more it eludes you. But when you are focussed on helping others from the goodness of your heart, watch how the money just comes to you. From a place of peace, you will make clearer decisions about what sort of house you want to buy, what investments you want to make, what type of work you should pursue and so on, because you are making them from a calm, clear mind, not from one that's busy, nervous or fearful. You will have no issues of self-worth because you will love and value yourself. Consequently, you will not get rid of any money that comes to you immediately because you will believe consciously and subconsciously that you are worth every penny and that you deserve it. You will decide wisely when you should use, save or share money.

Many people who come across money and don't value themselves tend to lose it pretty quickly through poor investments, gambling or other foolish choices of that nature. The last time I checked the statistics, 87% of people who win the lottery completely used up or lose the money within eighteen months of winning it. This is because they didn't believe they were worthy of the money. When they won the lottery, their system went into shock because something had happened that was out of their comfort zone, something they had never expected, something that had never happened to them before. So without realising it, these people felt the need to get rid of this unexpected reward—to vanquish the uncomfortable sense of disbelief that something like that would actually happen to them.

Many people chase money thinking that it will give them peace. Canadian actor and film producer, Jim Carrey, once said, "I wish everybody could be rich and famous and get everything they want so that they could realise that's not the answer". There is nothing inherently wrong with money itself. Money can give you more options in life and empower you to fulfil your dreams and help others. However, when you experience inner peace, you will no longer be held back by an attachment to money. You will simply be focussed on serving people and making a difference on the planet. And if you do that, I promise you, money will never be a concern for you.

I'm not saying that you'll be a multimillionaire. However, just serve the greatest number of people you can, doing what you do, using your unique set of skills, your unique product or service, then watch how you will never have to worry about money again.

When you realise that money is not the key to happiness or inner peace, you'll be able to appreciate and have fun with it, even give more away to help others. You will realise you don't need to feel guilty about owning luxury items; you will just appreciate them without being attached to them. You will realise that you are allowed to have those things: go on holidays, have a nice house and drive a nice car; however, your sense of worth and value as a person will not be attached to those objects. They will simply be temporary things that you can appreciate in your life for a time being but that you know will eventually pass on to another place just as everything in this world does.

Despite this, as I have walked my personal path of peace in my life, I find that I want less and less. The more I find inner peace and the more I practise all the things I'm going to teach you, the fewer things I want. However, that doesn't stop me from wanting a nice house for my family, that they can feel proud about and live comfortably in.

The money that flows from inner peace and from serving others will allow you to attend seminars or motivational workshops that you may be interested in. It will allow you to research and spend more time practising the activities or work that you love. The money will allow you to expand your business or grow in your career. The money will also allow you to travel more with your family and see the world and experience new things. You will be able to eat out at the best restaurants and travel with your friends. It will allow you to look after yourself with a gym membership or perhaps some exercise equipment for your home. You will be able to afford high-quality food for yourself and your family so that you can eat well and live strongly.

Inner peace will have a great impact on your family life. The analogy I give for this is the following: If you have a barking dog, the worst thing you can do to calm it down is bark back at it. When a dog has been abused or doesn't trust people, it's always on edge; it's always ready to bite and defend itself. However, just watch what happens to that dog when you are calm around it and only show it love. The animal changes completely.

The exact same goes for human beings. You will find that when you've found inner peace and you are radiating a different energy, the people who you used to clash with and have tension around will change also. They will sense that you are no longer a threat or that they can't get a reaction from you anymore from pushing your buttons. When you create this loving, peaceful space in your home, just like with the dog, the people around you will become completely different; they will relax and feel safe and comfortable just being themselves around you. Since they will not feel threatened, they will feel no need to defend themselves or start drama to vie for attention.

The truth is this path to inner peace is really quite simple. The greatest impact you can have on your family is not through what you tell them but by taking the action to transform yourself first; then you will be able to sit back and watch as other people transform around you.

My relationship with my father used to be a very tense one. I was always on edge around him, waiting for him to criticise and I would snap every time he did. I didn't have the awareness at the time to realise that my father just didn't like himself and the way he acted around me was an unconscious attempt for him to make himself feel better. Once I realised this, I saw how the way my father was actually benefitted me: It helped me to be an independent person growing up; it helped me to grow stronger and it led me to a place that I learned a lot from.

When I reached a place of peace and was able to transform my life, my family began to change around me because I was no longer a threat to them in terms of reaction and anger. They became calmer around me. My relationships with my family have grown to the point where there is nothing but peace and calm when we are together and we get along very well; even my father has changed because of this. He may not be sure why or how it has happened but he has become a much nicer person around me because he sees that I love myself. When he says or does something that I may have previously taken offense to, I don't react anymore; I stay calm.

The greatest gift you can give to your family is for you to find peace. Once you find peace within, you don't need to preach anything. Just live your life and trust that your family is going on their own journey, their own path. Some of your family members might not be ready to take the leap. Some may have a few more lessons to learn, a few more stepping stones to skip through.

Some might be causing drama for other people which may in turn help others to wake up. Just trust that whatever path they are on is their path and you don't need to try and force them onto your path.

One of the greatest things I've been able to witness in my life is seeing my family become a closer, more peaceful unit; seeing my younger siblings—even the oldest siblings—realise that maybe they don't know everything and taking their first steps into spiritual journeys of their own.

By finding inner peace, not only will you be helping your immediate family, you will be breaking the cycle for future generations to come. You will be showing your family the template for inner peace and balance so your future children and grandchildren will never know what it's like to have lives filled with drama and suffering. You will be teaching them a simple way to be at peace, a simple way to see the beauty in life and a simple way to see God all around us. By being a living, breathing example and role model for your family, you will be actively mentoring future generations of your family towards a place of peace, productivity and success.

When you don't love yourself, it's very difficult to have a calm, balanced family life. When you can't read the subtitles, it's very hard for you to not react negatively when seemingly bad things happen. When you are not aware of your thoughts, it's very hard to be at peace with yourself and your life. You get lost in your mind and then you are not able to be there for your children or your spouse when they need you and the quality of your relationships decreases. When you aren't able to be present, people don't feel like you are really there for them, giving them 100% of your attention.

However, when you can love yourself and see the beauty and the perfection to life, the quality of your relationships with family and friends will only continue to increase. You will feel more love than you've ever felt before toward your family and they will feel more loved by you and more love toward you in return.

A young man I coached recently had a major charge around his mother. They would clash constantly when they were in each other's presence. They also worked together, which made things even more difficult. However, there was a lesson in it for him. To his credit, he said, "John, I'm willing to do whatever it takes", and he ticked every one of the boxes in the action steps of the Five Keys system. Once he realised how simple the steps were, he was able to commit very quickly. Within only five sessions, this young man had gone from being angry and frustrated with his mother to seeing the perfection in why she is the way she is. As we came towards the end of the coaching, he said to me, "My mother's changed. I mean, she hasn't really done anything differently; it's just that *I've* changed. I've become calmer. She doesn't feel that I'm a threat anymore and as such, a nicer part of my mother comes out more often. I get it now. I realise that I can't wait for the world to change, rather, I have to be the change that I want to see in the world."

This young man is now also a role model for his younger sister who can see that he's taken the simple action steps and become a master of his emotions. Consequently, he's starting to master his life. The wonderful thing about this young man is he has found a passion for what he really loves and has realised through using his unique talents, he can be of service to others. He's out there doing it right now, slowly transitioning from his old job into doing what he loves most so that he can make the greatest difference in the world.

Inner peace will also transform your social life. When you go out socially, it won't be about quantity anymore—how often you go out. Instead, the quality of the time you spend with your friends will increase. Your friends will love being around you when you are radiating inner peace and self-love. You will be teaching them without them even realising it. You will be showing them that there is a way out of their depression, a way out of their anxiety, a way out of their unacceptance of themselves or others. Just being in your presence will elevate them to a higher level of awareness. When you go out with your friends, it's going to be a lot more fun now. You will see the joy, the beauty, the innocence in simply enjoying each other's company and having a good time. You will understand the futility of worrying about life. Consequently, you can have more laughs, more great times and a genuine connection with your friends, making memories that will last and bring you closer together. You may find that the number of people you truly call friends will decrease but you will have relationships of much higher quality with the friends you do have as you focus on fostering those connections without spreading yourself too thin.

The greatest gift you can give to your friends is to become a living example of inner peace. When somebody transforms in front of their eyes, they have to be startled. They have to want to ask questions. They may not take the actions steps for themselves immediately but those who are ready will ask you. Remember, when the student is ready, the teacher will appear.

Finally, when it comes to the Physical area of your life, inner peace will allow you to thrive. Your energy will flow naturally just as it should, as a car that gets regular servicing runs smoothly and effectively. A car that's looked after tends not to break down as often. The Five Keys to Inner Peace are your regular tune-ups that will keep your body flowing so that there are fewer breakdowns. Just realise that illness is not really a disease; it's the body's way of telling you that something's not quite right with you; that you have either a surplus or insufficiency of something. So if you are someone who's had regular health problems, know right now that you do not need to struggle to fight the illness. Health and healing should not require struggling because this often increases the intensity of the problem or creates new ones entirely. Take the action steps to the Five Keys of Inner Peace then watch how your body naturally heals itself. Your immune system will rise because you will no longer be beating yourself up. You will no longer be draining yourself mentally wondering why people are the way they are or letting others' opinions drag you down. When you are free of stress and anxiety, your body will respond accordingly and will begin to heal itself from the inside out.

When you are working in a job or career that inspires you, you may even find that you are capable of working twelve-hour days without a problem if you have to. Your sleep will be more restful. In fact, you will sleep better than you have ever slept and because of that, your body will be much better able to regenerate itself. Your vitality will be at an all-time high and you will radiate this positive energy.

Your self-love and inner peace will have you looking and feeling ten years younger. You will have the energy to exercise regularly, whether it be swimming or walking or dancing—whatever it is that you enjoy. You will see that you are able to find fun in the way you exercise. You won't be training so hard and burning yourself out in a desperate attempt to get people to love you for your appearance. You will just realise that you love life and the vehicle that you are travelling in, your body, needs to be looked after so that you can live a longer, more fruitful life. With your body running so happily and healthily, think of how much money you will save on medications and days off work. It's only going to bring more abundance to you.

When people come to me for coaching, I don't attempt to fix the symptoms of problems in the seven areas of life. Some people come and say to me, "I want help with my learning strategies so I can do better in my academics". Some people say, "I've no idea what I want to do for work. I need help choosing a career". Others will tell me, "My money situation is terrible and I want to improve that". Some will come to me because their relationships have broken down with family members or their spouse. Some people feel isolated and disconnected from friends and would like to improve that while still, others come to me wanting to improve their physical health.

Now, while it would be more financially beneficial for me to work on one area at a time with my clients and to go at things slowly, I don't deal with the symptoms. I have no interest in providing temporary fixes for problems that will only continue to arise once the coaching ends. When I teach the Five Keys to Inner Peace, I am targeting the core of what is going on with you. Once you have inner peace, all these areas of your life will start to improve. So you don't need to work on your spirituality, your intellectuality, your finances, your physicality, your social life or finding the perfect career. All you need to focus on right now is taking the simple action steps towards inner peace and watch how every part of your life will naturally begin to transform in turn.

You will feel connected to the Source of Life. You will feel that you are a genius and can apply your wisdom and knowledge to whatever it is that you want to learn. You will become an expert in your field. More work will naturally flow to you. Money will be there in abundance because you are serving people from the goodness of your heart and your family and friends will transform around you as they witness your transformation. Your health will be at an all-time high. You will be flourishing and vibrant. You will be more energetic than ever, and you will be truly making a difference on this planet that will go way beyond your mortal life.

~ *Chapter Four* ~
VALUES

It's not hard to make decisions once you know what your values are. ~ Roy E. Disney

Before I outline the action steps of the Five Keys to Inner Peace, I want to get you thinking about your values, the things in life you place the most importance on. Figuring out what you value most in your life will help give you a certain sense of direction after you have completed the action steps, found your place of inner peace and want to begin working towards your goals. It will give you a clearer picture of who you are. Knowing yourself better will give you clarity concerning the reasons for why you may have a tendency to make certain mistakes repeatedly, fall into certain habits or react in certain ways to some situations. Knowing yourself and your values better will help you to understand how you can channel your energy in the most beneficial ways.

To determine what you value most in life, you just need to ask yourself the right questions. I was able to learn from a great teacher, Dr John Demartini, at least thirteen questions you should ask yourself that will help you pinpoint the things you value most in each area of your life.

Get a pen and paper to keep track as we go along. Write the questions and then your answers under each.

The first question is: *How do I fill my space?* If somebody came over to your house and even took a peek inside your car, what would they notice? What are the top three things they would notice you seem to be really into? Think about this for a second and then write down the top three.

The next question is: *How do I spend my free time?* Think about the top three things you actually do in your life when you have time to yourself to do anything you like and write those down.

The third question is: *How do I spend my money?* I'm not talking about the things you spend your hard-earned money on out of necessity but rather, the things you spend your dough on when you've got extra to spend on things. Maybe it's collectible car models; maybe it's sport equipment; perhaps it's movies or books or music. Take a moment to think about this and write down your top three.

Question Four: *Where am I most reliable in my life?* Write down the top three areas in your life in which you are most reliable. Are you reliable when it comes to business or money? Maybe you are reliable in your family or your social life? Think about when and where you are the most dependable for others. When can you be counted on absolutely to follow through on something or provide service in something? Where do you have the most reliability?

Question Five: *In which area of my life am I most organised, disciplined and focussed?* Is it in spirituality? Is it in your research or with your studies? Is it in your job? Is it with family? Is it with making money? Where do you have the most discipline and focus? Write down your top three.

Question Six: *What do I think about most?* What are the thoughts that play through your head most often, on a day-to-day basis? What do you think a lot about? Is it about making money? Is it about your family, your partner? What are the top three things you think about every day?

Question Seven: *What is my self-talk?* What do you talk to yourself the most about from day to day? What are the top three things you tell yourself? Do you tell yourself you are a star and have the confidence to achieve whatever you want in life? Do you tell yourself you are going to be a computer programmer one day, or an award-winning actress? Do you tell yourself you need to do better in your relationships with others or in your studies? Think about the self-talk that goes through your head the most (or perhaps that you speak out loud to yourself) and write down the top three things that come to mind.

Question Eight: *What do I talk to others about most?* What are the top three things you love talking about and tend to turn conversations towards when speaking with others? Do you really enjoy talking about football; dogs; fashion? Write down your top three topics of conversational interest.

Question Nine: *What do I visualise the most?* What are the top three things you tend to visualise in your mind's eye? What are the movie scenes you play over again in your head? What kind of places do you visualise yourself travelling to or the things you imagine yourself doing one day? Top three. Write them down.

Question Ten: *How do you spend your energy?* What do you invest most of your energy into? What areas of your life would you like to invest more energy into? Is it towards making sure your children are doing well at school, pursuing your next promotion at work or building a favourite hobby of yours? What are some things you know you could do every day because you just love doing them so much? Write down the top three things you would like to invest your energy into on a daily basis, even if you aren't able to do so currently.

Question Eleven: *What inspires me the most?* Are there some great persons in history you see as role models? Are there particular people in your life who inspire you? Are there books you read or songs you listen to that get you inspired? Do you feel most inspired while camping in the mountains or in a cosy, bustling kitchen? Write down the top three people, places, activities or things that inspire you more than anything else.

The twelfth question is: *What do I set goals towards the most?* What are the top three things you set your life goals towards most frequently? Is it saving money? Does it have to do with business? Does it have to do with relationships? What are the top three areas in your life in which you most often set goals for yourself?

And the final question: *What do I love researching most?* When you walk into a bookstore or surf the Web in your free time, what are the top three things you are most interested in researching? What subjects really capture your attention and prickle your curiosity? What do you love absorbing information about, be it by reading, listening or watching?

Once you have three answers for each of these questions, tally them all up and take a look at which answer seemed to occur most often, second most often, and third most often. By looking at these answers, you should be able to get a pretty clear picture of the things in life you place the highest value on. Where you place your values will essentially determine what you do with your life.

What things in life are you absolutely passionate about? What things in your life are you willing to invest countless hours of time and energy on? What things are you willing to be patient and work hard to achieve or maintain? This is all about getting really clear about what it is that grabs your attention because if you don't live by your highest values, you will gravitate towards the animal in you, the quick fix, looking for a way to get yourself to feel better temporarily without ever fulfilling your ultimate goals and desires. This can only result in confusion and unhappiness.

Once you are clear about what your top highest values are, you will start to feel alive and fulfilled. You will be clearing away the fog that shrouds the pathway you must follow through life in order to achieve true peace and fulfilment. If you are not doing what you love in your life, you will not love your life.

No two people will have the same set of values, just as everyone has their own unique set of fingerprints. We are all individual; we are all unique; we all have our own set of values. Getting clear about what yours are will give you so much more clarity. When you start to get clear about what it is that you value most, you can start to shape your life around that. You need not feel any shame or guilt around them. Your values are just your values; they are neither right nor wrong though they may greatly differ from someone else's.

When I went through this process myself, I found that the answers I got most frequently pointed me in one direction. I ended up with a list that essentially told me what I wanted to do with my life, and that was to serve people by educating and inspiring others to make a difference on the planet. I realised that my absolute number one goal is to educate and inspire people. I also noticed that my second highest priority was researching into human potential and 'cracking the code' of life. As you can see Number Two was rather essential to achieving Number One. Number Three was my family and Number Four was travelling.

After getting clear about what my values were, I prioritised. The first thing I turned my attention to was Value Number One: Inspiring and educating others to live peaceful, productive and fulfilling lives. So I began researching into how I could do that. I wanted to learn from the greatest teachers on the planet. I wanted to expand my knowledge and become as familiar as I could with this field so that I would eventually be able to compile what I believed were all the best ways to achieving this. I wanted to become an expert in the subject so I would best be able to serve others through my passion. I loved talking to other people, hearing about their experiences and what they thought were some of the best ways to get the most out of life. I gladly spent my money on the learning I gained from workshops as I trained alongside other people who shared my enthusiasm and goals. Since then, I have filled much of my personal space with materials on how to get the most out of human beings and to live an inspired life.

Now just as with my values, some of you may realise that family did not come out on top of the list when you tallied up your answers and you may initially experience some guilt around this. However, there is no need to feel any shame or guilt. If everybody had family as their highest value, I believe there would be far less entrepreneurs in the world to create work and jobs for families and to create better lives for people overall through the services and products they provide. If everybody had family as their highest value, we wouldn't get much done in this world. I think we would miss out on a lot of the innovative services and products that are on the marketplace today. You need to realise that if your highest priorities are to serve others, you will be helping your family anyway.

My highest priority is to educate and empower people, including my family members, to live inspired lives and part of that involves putting in long hours at work. However, the money I make from the services I provide helps my family to be able to have the lifestyle they want while we're still able to spend quality time together. We appreciate the time we spend together more and because of this, we are able to bond closely as a unit. My family knows they have a father and a husband who is at peace and living an inspired life doing what he loves. They are comfortable and at peace around me and I am able to inspire them to also follow their dreams and reach their full potentials. I think you would agree that it's a lot easier to live with that kind of person than with someone who spends a lot of time with you but is not living their life according to their highest values. Someone who is resentful of their life or harbours regret and remorse about all the things they have not accomplished is not an easy person to be around.

Now that you are clear about what you value most, you are going to have a compass to guide you in the direction you want to head in life and what you would like to really invest your time in. The priority here is to get very clear on what that direction is. Don't feel any shame or guilt; just know that these are your values and *own* them. Everybody has their own set of values. Much of our frustration in life comes from trying to live by somebody else's values or trying to get other people to live by ours. Simply accepting others for who they are and understanding that their values are neither good nor bad, just like your own, can save you a lot of stress and heartache.

When it comes to values, you need to understand there are two sides to the equation. On one side, we have what we call the Golden Values or the values we love to share with other people. Typically, these values will look a lot like freedom, love, research and knowledge, making a difference on the planet, respect, generosity, service for others and so on.

As I learned from Ben Harvey, there is another side to the equation called the Shadow Values. For every Golden value, there's a Shadow opposite. The shadow side to love is attention. This is the value of the ego, the five-year-old, *I need attention first before I can get love.* Think about it; how can anybody love you if you don't have their attention? The Shadow Values are the things the ego wants. Since the ego is a part of all of us, we will always have a certain need to fulfil these Shadow Values. The trick is satisfying this need while maintaining a healthy balance between the Shadow and Golden Values in our life.

The Shadow Value to the Golden Value of freedom is control. The five-year-old ego wants control before you can have freedom. How can you have freedom in your life if you have no control? You may find that you feel the need to gain control over other people in certain situations and quickly get frustrated when you aren't able to do this. When this happens, all you need to do is shift that need for control over other people to a different area of your life. You can now channel that value towards a sense of control and responsibility over the things you *can* control such as your own choices and actions. I have started to realise that if I take more action towards serving rather than controlling other people, I have greater control over all seven areas of my life.

I have also realised that the flipside to my value for serving and inspiring others is the need to feel superior because my ego naturally wants to feel better than other people. What I have to do is calmly assure my ego: *You are going to get that feeling of superiority if you let me serve and inspire others first then your Shadow Value will be met and fulfilled.* That need for a sense of superiority only gives me further motivation to work towards studying, researching and gaining experience in the subjects I wish to teach to others so that I may inspire them.

For my Golden Value of wanting to research and learn more about unlocking one's full potential, the opposite Shadow Value is for the need to be right. If a part of me didn't have this need to be right, I wouldn't be so driven to learn new things. I wouldn't have the motivation to seek out the highest quality and most beneficial information I can find so that I can be right about the things I teach or at least, be a dependable source of information on the subjects I am passionate about. Being right about the things I love can help me share the most helpful ideas and advice with others so that they can gain something from my knowledge and experience.

As you can see, there is no good or bad, rather, there are simply two sides to every equation. You cannot have one without the other. So rather than feeling shame about the need to be right, we must realise that it serves a purpose in our life.

When you say you value honesty or respect, the Shadow Value for that is validation. Your need for validation, for people to say you are worthy, is what gives you the respect and the honesty you desire.

A lot of people say that they would really love to make a difference on the planet by sharing and giving away more money to help others. The Shadow Value to this Golden Value for generosity and service to others is money and anyone who says they don't value money or disowns the concept of money is, in essence, cutting off one of the ultimate sources to helping more people. How can you give more away if you are not able to create more? Through the natural abundance that flows from a place of inner peace you will be creating more money and in turn, you will be able to help more people, including your own family. Once you realise that money is a tool, an exchange for service, an exchange of love and appreciation, you will stop feeling guilt or shame around the fact that money is something that drives and motivates you. When someone says to you, "Thank you so much for doing that for me. Here's some money as a token of my love and appreciation", they are simply expressing their gratitude towards you for the service you provided them and repaying you with something that will be useful to you in your own life.

You don't need to feel ashamed that you value money. You just need to own up to both sides of the equation and get them to start working together for you.

Once I dissolved any lingering shame or guilt around the Shadow Values, I realised I needed to appeal to the five-year-old in me, my ego. I needed to convince my ego that the actions I take in life towards fulfilling my Golden Values are going to serve its needs and values also. To do this, I took, for example, my tutoring business and made a list. The first item I wrote down on this list was how growing my tutoring business would bring me more attention. As I put together this list, I scanned all the seven areas of my life.

I asked myself, *How will growing my tutoring business bring me more attention spiritually?* I answered that it would give me more attention in the spiritual field of life as I would start to become recognised as a spiritual teacher and looked up to for help and advice in my field of expertise.

Through growing my tutoring business, I would gain attention in the intellectual area of my life because I would be researching into how to get the most out of people and would be developing strategies to help people put this information to use in their lives. Thus, I would get more attention from the education industry through teaching the principles I want to share with others so they can get the most out of their lives.

If I grew my tutoring business, I could actually create more work for myself and for other people, and that would bring me attention from other people in the industry as they notice that my business is truly helping others and I am providing a valuable service through my work.

Growing my business would also bring me attention financially. I'd have more attention from financial advisors, from banks, from people in general, because in this world, who isn't attracted to money flowing in abundance? As I would start to make more money, people would take notice and wonder how I did it. They would be curious and want to know more, and I would get attention because of this and hence, have even greater opportunities to share my strategies.

I would also receive more attention from my family once they realised that our quality of life would be improving and it would be coming from the growth of the business.

Growing my business would bring me more attention from my friends who would notice my success and want to know my 'secret'. They would stop and wonder, *Wow, if he can do it, why can't I?* And once again, I would be given the opportunity to share my strategies with them so that they could find the same success and fulfilment.

Finally, I convinced my ego that by taking action and growing my tutoring business, I would be getting attention physically. Since I would be doing what I am truly passionate about, I would have more vitality, more energy than ever, which would help me physically; I would have less illness and greater strength. I would have the energy to exercise. I would have the energy to put long hours into the work I love and would be more productive than ever. I would have the motivation to take care of my body and once I do that, people would notice and think, *Wow, he looks great for his age!*

Once I went through all seven areas of my life, appealing to my ego, reassuring it that its Shadow Values would be more than taken care of, I could turn back again to the Golden Values. I could remind myself of the true reason why I am doing all that I am doing and just how important my Golden Values are in driving me to lead a happy, successful life making a difference in the world.

The opposite of attention is love. So I went over how growing my tutoring business was going to bring me more love in the spiritual realm. By growing my business, not only would I really feel a sense of peace knowing that I would be helping more people to live an inspired life, I would receive love in return from those people. They might say, "Thank you John for helping me get to this place of peace and balance". They would be expressing their love and gratitude to me by saying this and that would bring me the love I want and value. I realised I would also receive help and love from the spiritual community that I would have become a part of as they would acknowledge and recognise my work.

I would receive love in the intellectual area of my life. People might say, "I love how you know that and are able to share it with me". I might have parents saying to me, "Thank you for helping my child free his life of drama and be successful at school and at home". Likewise, the adults I coach and attend my workshops might say, "I really love what you are doing. Thank you for sharing your knowledge with us and using your talents for good".

I would see more love through being able to make more money as I grow my business because I would be able to help more people. The more I would have, the more I would be able to give away. I would be able to show people that there's a way of making money through doing something that you love. I would receive more love from my family, from my wife and kids for being able to provide them a life they've always wanted and afford vacations to new places where we could experience new things together and bond as a family. I would also get love from my extended family, from my in-laws, when they see that I was providing a really comfortable life for their daughter and their grandkids.

I would also get a lot of love from my friends from growing my tutoring business. They might say, "Thank you. You are inspiring me to take action and do the same. It's really great what you are doing".

And finally, I knew I would be receiving plenty of love physically because I would be happy; I would be healthy; I would be vibrating a different energy, radiating peace and calm. I would look and feel a lot more attractive.

The process is all about appealing to your ego whenever there is something you want or need to do so that you can get it on board to work with you rather than against you. Go through the seven areas of your life and explain to that five-year-old how it is going to have its Shadow Values fulfilled and it will be more than willing to help you along the journey rather than holding you back.

What I did with attention, I also did with control by answering my ego's question, *How is growing my business going to bring me more control?* Once again, I begin with the first area of my life and worked my way down to the seventh, appealing to my ego, reassuring it that by growing my tutoring business I would gain more control over all areas of my life. I assured it that I would have more control over how I feel spiritually, more control over what and how often I can learn by attending certain workshops or seminars. I would gain greater control over where, when, how much and how often I work, as well as who I work with. Expanding my business would give me a lot more control over my finances and hence where I live, the car I drive, how often I can travel, the education I can give my kids and so on. Growing my business would bring me greater control over my family life because of the increased flexibility in my work life, I would be able to spend more time with my family, take them on holidays more often and give them the life they really want. Likewise, I would gain greater control over my social life and how often I get to spend time with my friends or am able to go away on holidays with my best mates. Lastly, expanding my business would give me greater control over my health because if I grew my speaking business, I would be living an inspired life every day and that would greatly increase my vitality and energy and thus, my physical wellbeing.

The flipside to control is freedom. So as my ego would be having all its needs met, I would be gaining what I really want, fulfilling my Golden Value of freedom. As I would have increased control over all areas of my life, this would in turn give me greater freedom to make the choices I want.

One of your ego's values may be the need for validation because validation brings you respect. So if this is a value of your ego, you would go through the seven areas of your life and explain to your ego how it would be getting validation through achieving your goals, which would in turn bring you respect.

Another Shadow Value that you might reconcile is the value for money. Most people I have met seem to disown the fact that they value money. However, if somebody offered you $100,000 to drive to their house at 3:00 o'clock in the morning, something tells me you would be there. So, what you need to do is appeal to your ego by saying: *Ego, we are going to make money in all areas of life by taking these actions. You will be able to get all the money you need to survive and more, so just relax.*

The Golden side to this value is generosity. The more money you make, the more money you can part with; the more money you can allow to flow into the economy to provide more jobs for more people, to allow people to grow financially in their own lives. There are many people on this planet who are generous and want to give but because they do not value money (or do not want to own up to the fact that they do) they are not allowing themselves to help as many people as they could if they let go of the shame around valuing it and start to be grateful for it instead. This is why it is important to be able to just own it. Don't feel any shame or guilt around the things you value. If you value money and want more of it, admit and confirm it with yourself. Trying to change any of your values is a difficult and often unnecessary battle. What you must do instead is be certain you are channelling your energy towards fulfilling your values in a way that helps you and others grow in all areas of life.

Another Shadow Value is sex. You may enjoy and value sex a lot yet find that it is something you sometimes feel guilty about. A part of you might be suppressing that or you may be lacking intimacy in your life. You must first own up to the fact that you value sex and it is important to you. Do not try to suppress your ego's value for it because your ego and its wants will be with you for the rest of your life. What you must do is learn to channel those needs to fulfil your goals and your Golden Values.

I have found that many people are ashamed of the entire subject of sex or think it's a taboo topic and have attached a shameful stigma to it. I have realised that many people would rather exclaim and highlight their value for love and say they want intimacy. But how can you have intimacy without valuing sex? It is the ego in us that says: *Get the quick fix; go out and have sex with whoever you want whenever you want.* It's also the animal instinct in us to reproduce so as to keep our species alive. Therefore, that animal part of you craves sex and is driven by a need for it. When you feel the ego rising up to complain that its need for sex is not being fulfilled, simply appeal to it by saying: *You know what, Ego? If we make a difference in other people's lives and establish a family of our own, if I'm supporting my partner's values and I'm helping them to fulfil those values, then they are going to want more intimacy which is going to, in turn, bring you more sex.*

It's all about getting really honest with yourself and realising that if you are dealing with any intimacy problems, it's probably because you have attached a negative or shameful stigma around sex. For you to bring more intimacy into your life, you will need to open up about the topic of sex and realise that you need both sides of that coin to have the intimacy you want, to fulfil your Golden Value. You cannot disown sex if you want intimacy. You cannot complain that you are lacking intimacy in your life if you are too embarrassed to admit that you value sex. The flipside to the value for sex is the Golden Value of intimacy. By reassuring your ego that it is going to have its need for sex fulfilled by the actions you wish to take in your life; your ego is going to, in turn, help you to gain the intimacy you desire in your life.

Again, when you convince your ego that by doing what you really want to do with your life, it is also going to have its Shadow Values met, it will be ready to climb on board. Otherwise, you are going to be wasting energy fighting against an undeniable part of you and searching for that single-sided coin that doesn't exist.

By the end of this process, you will see that both sides of you win. You have successfully sated your ego so that it willingly works with you in your life's missions rather than inhibiting you from achieving your goals. It is in the passenger seat and you are in the driver's seat, in charge of your life and ready for whatever comes your way.

So just get clear about your Golden and Shadow values, then take it a step further by prioritising. Figure out which of these values you value the most. Is it freedom? Is it love? Is it inspiring people? Is it education? Is it respect? Whatever they are, just understand that if those are your three or four highest values, then your highest Shadow Values will be the opposite sides and cannot be denied or disowned.

There is a strategy you can use to help you get really clear about which exactly your Shadow Values are and this is by paying attention to the things that bother or annoy you the most. The next time you are in a situation where you find yourself getting really upset or frustrated, just stop and ask yourself, *What is it that I'm not getting at this moment? Which of my values is not being fulfilled?* If you are honest with yourself, you will find that perhaps you are not getting enough attention, you don't have control of the situation, you don't feel superior, you aren't getting validated, you don't have enough money or you were wronged in that situation while having to admit that somebody else was right. Therefore, just pay attention to what bothers you the most and this will help you to figure out which are your highest Shadow Values.

When going through this process myself, I noticed that I'd get annoyed sometimes if I felt I wasn't getting attention from somebody. I also became perturbed when I felt I didn't have control over certain things. When I began teaching in elementary schools and was told, "You can't do this... You can't do that... This is against regulations... We have rules for these things", I would get frustrated pretty quickly. I realised I needed control over how I teach in order to be able to try new things and discover the best ways to teach and help children grow.

I also noticed that my need to be right has brought me to argue with people often. However, once I became aware of that, I was able to start shifting my energy towards researching into the things I wanted to become an expert in to enable me to help more people by sharing that knowledge. Additionally, I noticed I have a need to feel superior because I felt anger and frustration when I felt that I was less than somebody else. However, once I became clearer on that, I was able to redirect the ego's need for those things towards serving a higher purpose.

Eventually, the attention I got from fulfilling my Shadow Values brought me more love. The control gave me more freedom. The need to be right pushed me to research more and learn from the greatest teachers on the planet, and the need to feel superior allows me to stand in front of thousands of people today to help them by sharing my knowledge and experience.

Now that we have a foundation built around what the ego is as well as the Golden and Shadow Values, the core of what really drives us as human beings, we're going to turn our attention to how these play a part in your journey towards inner peace and achieving balance and abundance.

If you become aware of your Shadow Values, you will stop using up your energy fighting against yourself, your ego, and will be able to put that energy towards fulfilling your Golden Values. When you remove any shame or guilt around your Shadow Values, you will be able to fulfil the Golden ones. You cannot have one without the other. This is a two-sided coin, so if you are looking for one side of the coin, you are going to feel frustrated because you will realise you can't find it without, still, being stuck with the opposite side. This is what you may be running into if you are experiencing frustration, shame or even depression in your life. There is a very good chance the issues stem from the fact that you are desperately struggling to fulfil one side while neglecting and denying the other.

If you don't go over this process with yourself, you're going to find that you are continually battling with yourself. You're going to find that you are your own worst enemy because the fact of the matter is, if you don't show your five-year-old ego that it's going to get attention by helping you live an inspired life, it's going to seek attention elsewhere. It's going to resort to any means to get it and it's going to do so, primarily, by creating drama. It's going to create drama in your relationships, in business, in money matters, at your work. The five-year-old is going to say: *Well, maybe we won't get any attention from doing anything else, but at least we're getting attention for this!* This is one of the main reasons why children tend to act up in school. They'd rather get negative attention that no attention at all because they know that if they are ignored, they cannot be loved.

By convincing the ego that you are going to get so much more attention from living your inspired life than what you will get out of your victim mentality, you will calm it right down and it will be content riding along in the passenger seat while it lets you do the driving. You just have to get it to see that people all around you are going to give you more attention from the change they see in you. They will say, "Wow, look at you! You've really changed. Tell me about how you did it!" You are going to get much more attention from a bigger audience and be living on a bigger stage. You will have all the attention you want from family, friends, partners, co-workers and strangers alike because they will be drawn to the peace, love and vitality you are radiating. All this will get you so much more attention than playing the victim and acting out drama in your life. Once you are aware that there is a part of you that is addicted to getting attention by creating drama, you can simply redirect it by showing and convincing that part of you that there is so much more attention waiting for you. Then once you have convinced the ego that there is more attention waiting for it, you are going to be able to receive more love.

I used to get very frustrated when I felt I didn't have control over a situation in my life and my ego wanted to create drama in reaction to that. I had to teach myself to calm my ego by saying: *Look, if you simply cooperate with me by helping me grow my business and help more people, you are going to have so much more control in all areas of your life. You are going to have so much more control over your own life as soon as you stop trying to control other people's lives.*

Once I showed my ego this, it was on board: *Wow, we're going to have so much more control than we've ever had by doing something that's inspiring.* Through that, I received so much more freedom. So the need for control allowed for the greatest freedom in my life to do what I want, which is to be able to get up every day and do what I love by serving more people in a way that is unique and true to me.

When your ego's need to be right initiates an argument with another person, instead of getting frustrated or angry, remind your ego: *Hey, we're going to feel even more right when we've researched into an area of life that we are really passionate about and we become an expert in that field. Let's redirect that need to be right into something that's going to serve us. And you know what? When you are doing a job you love and making a difference in other people's lives, you are going to feel more superior than you have ever felt before without having to try and make others look small in order for you to look bigger.*

Focus on growing yourself bigger and better rather than pushing others down to give the illusion of your own greatness. Pushing others down or playing small to try and illicit attention doesn't serve anybody, and if it works, it is merely a temporary fix. By growing yourself to be the best person you can be, someone who serves people and shows them the way they can live inspired lives of their own, your ego's value for superiority is going to be fulfilled as you are able to pass on your knowledge to others in a meaningful and helpful way.

When children or teenagers act up at school or at home, this is often due to their need for attention and love. If they are lacking attention, they will feel they are lacking love. To help children with this, you can explain to them how, by turning their lives around, they're going to get so much more attention from their teachers, from friends, from family—people won't believe how much they have changed and will give them more attention, and they are just going to get a lot more love in their lives.

Likewise, talk to your ego like it's a five-year-old and convince it that there are good things coming its way if it can help you redirect your Shadow Values into a higher purpose, into a better form.

Taking Action

On the mornings of most days of the week, I go to a pool and swim laps for exercise and to have some time to myself. During this hour or so every morning, I take time to go over all my lists in my head. First, I go over the list of the things I love about myself and the things I am grateful for in my life. Then I go over my list of my highest Golden and Shadow Values. I go over how growing my tutoring and speaking business or training teachers is going bring me more attention, more control, make me feel more right and superior in my life, which on the flipside, is going to bring me more love, give me more freedom, the time to research into human potential and to empower people to live inspired lives.

I encourage you to do the same. After going through the process outlined in this chapter and making your lists, keep them somewhere close to you where you will be reminded of them every day. Place them in your electronic devices with reminders to read them daily. Eventually, you will carry them with you in your mind and be able to go over them every day without needing to look at your lists. Choose a particular time during your routine that works for you; perhaps while riding the bus to work, taking your dog for a walk or going to the gym.

Go over your lists regularly and remind yourself, both your Golden Values and your Shadow Values are a part of who you are—a two-sided coin that cannot be separated. Own up to who you are, to every side, to every angle and know that you need both sides of the equation to equal a loving, balanced and productive human being.

~ *Chapter Five* ~

TRACKING YOUR PROGRESS

A little progress everyday adds up to big results. ~ Satya

You are about ready to begin unlocking the secret of the Five Keys to Inner Peace. However, before you walk out your door and set foot on the path, turn to the back of this book where you will find a progress report in the form of a simple chart with six weeks on it and different sections for each Key. As you go through the processes in this book and take the action steps towards your goals, you can use this report as a way for you to keep written track of your progress, which you will be able to review as you go along. This will provide you with a visual reminder that will serve as extra motivation whenever you look at the numbers and see how far you have come since you began your search for inner peace.

You will see on the chart that you have an area to fill out at the beginning of each section. Before you take the action steps to each Key, give yourself an initial score from 0 to 10 in each area. So for the statement "I love myself unconditionally", give yourself a score from 0 to 10; zero being you do not love yourself unconditionally and ten being that you feel you absolutely love yourself unconditionally. As you go along and learn of each new Key, give yourself an honest score of where you feel you are at before beginning to implement the Key in your life. Later on, you will be able to see just how far you have come as you keep track of your progress by scoring yourself again each week.

When working with my clients, I love seeing the numbers, the actual data. I do this with everyone I coach, keeping the scores stored in a folder. At the end of their coaching with me, I show them their scores and how much they have changed. Many are astonished to realise that they started with threes in some columns and now they're rating themselves nine out of ten.

As you start to fulfil every area of your life, you are going to find that the effects will spill over onto all other people that you meet. So you will be not only benefitting yourself, you will be helping so many other people who may be watching and observing as they come into contact with you. They will notice that you are an inspired person living with purpose and they will become inspired by that. You will truly make a difference by being fulfilled in all areas of your life. An inspired person, a person who has fulfilment, makes a massive difference on the planet. The effect of their mortal life goes well beyond their death. You will not only be creating a better life for yourself but for people that you meet. You will be leaving behind a legacy that will stand the test of time. The effect of your teachings, your products or your services will go on into eternity.

~ *Chapter Six* ~

THE FIRST KEY TO INNER PEACE: LEARNING TO LOVE YOURSELF

*True love is easy to find... Look in the mirror and love yourself
and love will shine on you forever. ~ Anonymous*

Before you can do anything else, you must learn to love yourself. This is crucial because you are always going to feel like something is missing until you learn to love yourself completely. You may have the job, you may have the relationship but you are always going to feel like there is one thing missing and this is that one thing.

Firstly, when I say, "Learn to love yourself", I don't mean narcissism, staring at yourself in the mirror all day admiring how beautiful you are, nor do I mean arrogance where you go around telling people that you are better than them. To love yourself is purely to wake up each and every day grateful to be you and not wanting to be anybody else. When I ask people I coach, "Could you write a list of fifty things that you love about yourself?" they usually give me a look that says *"I don't think I could think of ten!"*

Quite often, it is this one missing thing that has brought these people to me searching for help in the first place. So many issues in our life can stem from the lack of this action. Before we can love others, we must learn to love ourselves first. Before we can be productive, helpful and useful in our lives, we must learn to love ourselves first. Before we can have peace in all areas of our life, we must learn to love ourselves first. Simply knowing how to do this (and then doing it) can clear up much of the drama and heartache we experience.

If you've noticed any three or four-year-olds around lately, you've probably realised that they don't have any self-esteem issues. They love life. They just go about their days with amazement and bewilderment at how wonderful life is and how much fun it is. You were that age too once. So what happened between then and now that you can't think of fifty things you love about yourself? This is what usually happened: You grew up around people, relatives, friends, classmates—general members of society—who sometimes said and did things, while they were letting the five-year-old ego control them, and you thought that maybe there was something wrong with you. Perhaps

Mum and Dad didn't love you the way you wanted to be loved or were simply bad at expressing it, so you would have thought, *Maybe there is something wrong with me—I mean, if my own parents can't truly love me, who's going to love me? Am I lovable?* Perhaps you came home from school when you were young and your parents said, "You are not coming first in school? What's wrong with you?" and you thought, "Maybe there is something horribly wrong with me. Maybe I'm broken."

Same too in the sporting field. Anytime you lost a game, people might have said, "Aw, you lost! What's wrong with you?" and again, that message of *"Maybe there is something wrong with me!"* would come flooding through your mind.

And then you would have discovered the television and in between your favourite TV shows are the commercials. These commercials usually convince and remind us constantly that there is something broken in ourselves or in our life, some kind of deficiency and that you or your life needs fixing. Of course, the advertising company supposedly has the product that will solve all your worries. This is the only way they can sell you anything, by getting you to believe you are incomplete or broken and need fixing.

The truth is, you are not broken, you don't need fixing; you are whole, you are not missing anything. However, if you don't learn to love yourself, it's a bit like putting an ad on the internet saying, "WANTED: SOMEBODY TO LOVE ME UNCONDITIONALLY FOR THE REST OF MY LIFE. I CAN'T DO IT, CAN YOU?"

I want you to do something now: Take a moment to make a list in your mind of your top three best friends.

Were you on that list? Probably not. Most people I ask this question look at me rather confused as if to say, *Why would I put myself on my own best friends list?*

I'm here to tell you now that your number one goal in life should be to make yourself your own best friend. What exactly does this mean? It means that you give yourself the same advice, care and love that you would give to your best friend.

When a good friend of yours is in trouble and comes to you needing help or looking for support and advice, you offer them whatever you can. But when the person in trouble is you or you've made a mistake and gotten yourself into a mess, you tend to kick yourself down. Being your own best friend is purely treating yourself the way you would treat your best friend.

So how do you go about loving yourself? It's not complicated and I like to use certain strategies to help the process along. When working with my clients, we come up with a list called *PPGG*. These letters stand for the four categories, *Physical, Personality, Good at?* and *Grateful for?*

Just take a moment now to grab a pen and paper and draw up four columns with those titles.

Under the first column, *Physical*, write down as many things as you can that you love about yourself in regards to your physicality. Scan yourself from top to toes: Do you like your hair? Your eyelashes? Your eyebrows? Your smile? Your dimples? Your freckles? Your ears? Your jaw line? Your lips? Your neck? Your arms? Your shoulders? Your height? Your laugh? Your voice? Your stamina? Your strength? Is it your legs? Your feet? Etc. Consider anything having to do with your physical body and write down those things that you love.

Once you've done that, move your attention to *Personality*. What do you love about your personality? You may find that it helps to go through the letters of the alphabet in your mind to help trigger words that you feel describe your personality. For example, for the letter *A*, perhaps you are adventurous, appreciative, ambitious or amusing. For *B*: Brave, bold, bashful, boisterous. For *C*: Compassionate, clever, curious. For *D*: Determined, dependable, discreet. For *E*: Energetic, efficient, enthusiastic, emotional, eclectic and so on. These are just examples to help get you thinking. Think of as many as you can that you believe apply to you and write down all the ones you love.

In the next column, write down everything that you are *Good At*. Start by scanning all seven areas of your life. Are you good at helping others spiritually? Do you excel in academic environments—when it comes to learning and education? Perhaps you are good with languages? What are you good at when it comes to work? Money: making or saving money? What about family and socially? Physically, are you good at sport? Are you good at music? Art? Fixing things? Are you good at swimming? Tennis? Juggling? Whistling? Think of anything that you know you are good at and write it down.

Finally, in the last column, write down everything that you are *Grateful For*. Again, scan the seven areas of your life. Are you grateful for going on a spiritual path to find inner peace? Are you grateful for particular spiritual teachers or mentors in your life? For particular books that you have read that helped you grow spiritually? Are you grateful for the ability to be able to learn anything you want? Are you grateful for any particular job or work that you have now or have had? Are you grateful for the money that you have in your bank account? Are you grateful for your family or certain family members in particular? Are you grateful for certain friends and friendships? Are you grateful for having all your limbs or being able to get around? Are you grateful for the house you live in? The car you drive? For having three meals a day on the table? Are you just grateful to be alive?

By the time you have done this, you should have at least fifty items in all four columns. Now store them in your tablet or your phone so that you will have them with you at all times. If you don't have a smart phone or a tablet, simply post your list on a wall near your bed, over your vanity or in your bathroom, somewhere you will see it every day. If you do have a smart phone or a tablet, go into your reminders or your calendar and create a new daily reminder with an alarm to go off once every morning and once every night, reminding you to read your list.

This is where the science comes in: Every time you read the things you love about yourself and what you are grateful for, your brain is going to release feel-good chemicals such as dopamine, serotonin and oxytocin. You may have heard depression defined as a chemical imbalance. Well, by reading your list and releasing these chemicals in your brain, your internal chemistry is going to get back into a balanced state, which will equal peace and contentment for you. I've worked with people who had depression and anxiety and were on medication who completely turned their lives around purely with this one simple action. Now if you currently take prescribed medication, I'm not recommending you to get off it right away. However, what I can tell you is that by consistently doing this task, your brain will release the chemicals that are generally found in the artificially manufactured pills you take, through your own body's natural processes and in their purest forms, and best of all, they are free and come with absolutely no negative side effects or risk of overdose.

The second simple task when it comes to learning to love yourself involves looking in the mirror. Once a day, you are to look at yourself in the mirror, maintaining your focus on your eyes and say, "I love you", "I love [your name]", and finally, "I love me", three times each. If you cannot look yourself in the eyes and say these things, you will never truly believe that anybody on this planet loves you.

If you do this, you will start to notice a sense of calm and gratitude entering your being; you will no longer be desperately seeking temporary fixes by chasing validation from external sources, which is far from a consistent or dependable solution. What many people confuse for genuine love is, in actuality, dependency. When you don't truly love yourself, you send out an energy, a vibe that says you are desperate, that you desperately need somebody to fill a void, that you are looking for a soul mate, somebody to save you.

I know this from personal experience. I went through a cycle of relationships over a period of time in my life during which I was desperately searching for somebody—for anybody—to make me feel better. But when none of my partners could make me feel whole, I ended up blaming and resenting them for my emptiness, which was due to incomplete awareness on my part.

Until you learn to love yourself completely, you are going to look for faults in your partner or in other people in your life, which can often lead to the breakdown of relationships. In the end, nobody is better off. You feel as empty and lonely as ever and your relationships suffer.

If you stop to observe your life and are honest with yourself, you will realise that most of what you do in your life is driven by the motivation to find some sort of love or validation. When I asked you to list your top three friends, did you notice that there are possibly some similarities between your friends and you, either personality-wise or in regards to interests? Can you see that you are trying to like and spend time with people who are similar to you in some ways, so that perhaps you can like yourself more or at least feel better about the things you do that might be deemed inappropriate by society?

My advice to you is to cut out the middleman and learn to love yourself without the help of others. Learn to realise just how magnificent you are and that nothing's missing and you are not broken. There are a lot of people out there desperately searching for love. As Mother Teresa puts it, "There are many in the world dying for a piece of bread but there are many more dying for a little love". What she meant by this was that although our basic needs for air, sleep, food and water must be met for us to remain physically well, there is something that drives us even more as human beings. The need for love is one that cannot be ignored lest the soul wither and cease to lend true vitality to the physical body we travel in. As human beings, we are hardwired to crave love and affection from other humans, and this need is no less important than the air we breathe.

Say there is a fellow who goes into a nightclub one weekend desperately searching for love. He really doesn't feel good about himself, so he is seeking out that one person whom he believes will make him feel whole. He goes into the nightclub and tries really, really hard, giving off the vibe that he desperately wants somebody. What happens is that most women are actually repelled, thinking, *If this guy desperately wants me to make him happy, I don't want that responsibility!*

It is a universal law that if you don't believe that you are lovable or that you are loved, then you are not going to find love. The universe can only give you what you already are, what you already have, and then multiply it. If you don't have self-love, it cannot give you true love through the form of another person.

Now, a person who has confidence in themselves, loves themselves and simply knows how to enjoy life, walks into the same night club; they would send out a completely different vibe that says *"I'm fine. I'm calm. In fact, I'm quite happy and I don't need anybody to make me feel good."* They would attract a variety of people towards them who want to be around the presence of someone so relaxed that made them feel comfortable and not threatened. From there, they would be in a really good position to choose who they felt would be a good partner for them—someone who was in a similar place in life as them.

A person who loves themselves and knows how to be confident and happy with who they are tends to attract people who notice this about them. They notice this confidence, this self-love, and would like to learn more about it or simply be around that positive energy because it is calming and makes them feel comfortable and relaxed. So the ultimate strategy really for finding the perfect partner is to learn to love yourself first. Once you remove the perceived notion that you are dependent upon finding somebody else to love you before you can be truly happy, just watch what happens. You will start to vibrate a different energy and people on a similar wavelength will pick up on that frequency and be drawn to you.

If you don't learn to love yourself, you are going to keep attracting similar partners or individuals who are also searching desperately for external validation and are dependent upon such as a solution to their unhappiness. I know this from first-hand experience. I was looking for people to save me because there was always this underlying fear I carried, that I was not good enough. So I looked for people who needed me more than I needed them. My reasoning was because they were so needy that there was less of a chance of them leaving me for somebody else.

Several relationships later, I realised an ugly pattern emerging in my love life. I finally got tired of this when I realised the amount of time and energy I was investing in these relationships were getting me absolutely no closer towards peace and happiness. So I made a conscious decision to be single for a while after my marriage broke down. During that time, I did some reflection and realised that because I didn't love myself, I kept getting myself involved in relationships that were ultimately doomed from Day One.

While I had stopped searching for someone to save me, a beautiful partner was being sent to me at a time that I was learning to love myself. When I first met my current wife, I said to her, "Be careful, I'm not ready for a relationship . . . Run!" But as I learned to love myself, I realised that the universe had sent me somebody who was calm, very confident in herself and didn't need anybody to make her feel lovable. We have been together since.

When it comes to teenagers, boys in particular, you will notice that a lot of them are drawn to computer games or to sports. The reason for this is because they feel they get love and attention for these activities. If a young boy is good at computer games, he gets high-fived. If he scores the winning goal in his team sport, he's hugged and given praise; his family and friends give him their approval and love. These boys don't get the same love and attention for doing well academically, which is why a lot of boys don't do so well in school.

When it comes to teenage girls, generally, many will drift towards the popular group because if they can be associated with the popular peers, that will give them more attention and supposedly, make them more lovable. Girls tend to out-perform boys when it comes to academics because they get recognition for it. They actually receive love and attention from other girls who value education and can see that through being well-educated, they're going to be able to live an independent and successful life. The values of boys and girls are different, thus they receive praise from success in different areas of life.

If you don't learn to love yourself, you may find that you become addicted at some level to social media sites. You will want to see just how many friends you can add and this will affect your contentment with your real-world social life and self-esteem because you need that external validation from other people to make you feel lovable. You could have hundreds of friends but sometimes it only takes one friend to 'de-friend' you to make you feel like your world's caving in.

Learning to love yourself makes *you* the only person that has to love you in order for you to feel whole, rather than waiting for a thousand people or for that one particular person to love you. It only takes *you* to love you for you to feel whole.

Class clowns who tell jokes to gain attention do so because it makes them feel valuable. They see that by being clever or funny they can attract people to them in some way and this makes them feel good about themselves—it makes them feel lovable. Guys who spend a lot of time in the gym may be driven by the same thing, the need to feel loved. They want to feel attractive; they want to be noticed. However, often attention is mistaken for its more meaningful and lasting counterpart, genuine love, and is only superficial and temporary. When people set their focus on external beauty, this is usually coming out of a place where they feel as though they're not lovable as a person or do not have an 'attractive' enough character. So they work on the shell, the external appearance. This is why physically attractive people throughout history, who have been known and loved for their beauty, have had a tendency to rely on their appearance to bring them success, love and attention. If you got love and attention for the way you look and you felt that it was the main reason why people loved you, wouldn't you do everything you could to preserve that? For this reason, we have so much plastic surgery for people. Celebrities and models in particular, tend to go to great lengths to preserve their beauty because deep down, they feel that if they don't stay physically attractive, people will stop noticing and loving them.

Unfortunately, beauty fades as does youth. If you don't have love for yourself, you will reach a point somewhere in your life when you realise that your external beauty has faded away and now something is missing; you will suddenly feel incomplete without it. Until you learn to love yourself, you may have an obsession at some level over your appearance and what people think of you so you will never truly feel at ease with who you are. This only adds extra stress to your life and can lead you to waste much time and money on trying to make yourself appear more loveable and attractive on the outside, which will only bring you temporary results.

When you do love yourself, you will age gracefully. You will have an aura about you, a beautiful energy that people will notice. You will attract people regardless of your age and your physical appearance. When it comes to physical beauty, I believe that whether you are an Adonis or a model, whether you are average looking or below-average looking, there is a spiritual path involved in each circumstance.

I was coaching a teenage girl who shared that she wasn't confident because she wasn't one of the 'popular' or 'pretty girls' at her school and she didn't like going out socially because of that. I was able to get her to see that because of her circumstances, she had been forced to look within herself and learn to love herself because she wasn't getting any attention from her physical appearance. Once she realised that and learned to love herself more because of who she was rather than the way she looked, she no longer wished that she was physically stunning nor had everyone turned their heads when she walked into a room. She understood that it was much more important for her to work towards developing her character so that she could be a beautiful person whom people would want to get to know and be around.

On the other hand, I've worked with many attractive women who get a lot of attention for their looks but said they had become sick of it. They said that because they had gotten so much attention their whole lives for their appearances from so many people that they had actually become bored when they realised it didn't fulfil them, that something was still missing. This forced them to look within themselves to search for that 'missing something' and to go on their own spiritual journey.

Therefore, whether you are physically attractive or not, the path to self-love is there, ready and waiting for you to take it. The most important thing is to be an attractive person from the inside out because that beauty lasts beyond a lifetime and will never fade nor cease to be attractive.

The thing is, when you learn to love yourself, you will truly begin to look more attractive. People notice it. People are drawn to it. Because you love yourself more and your self-esteem is at a healthy level, you will want to take better care of yourself and pay more attention to what you eat and how much exercise and sleep you get. The healthier your mind is, the healthier your body can become. You will simply have a glow about you that says "*I am confident. I love myself. I am at peace.*" You will find that this attracts not only attention but also genuine love towards you; you will be fulfilled through the meaningful relationships you are able to make because of this. You will not only appear more physically attractive but your personality will shine with your newfound confidence and calm demeanour.

When you learn to love yourself through the simple actions of reading your list and looking in the mirror daily to say, "I love you", you will begin to feel a sense of calm coming from within, a sense of completeness, that nothing is missing, that you are not broken and you don't need fixing. From this will come a more centred and balanced person who is able to take control of their emotions. You will stop chasing love, rather, you will have love follow you. You will be in no hurry to find the right partner for yourself, you will just be content knowing that you already love yourself; you are whole and your life is fine just the way it is and can only get better from here. Then when the time is right, a person who also loves themselves and is at peace will come along for you.

If you don't learn to love yourself, you are going to be prone to 'falling in love'. Falling in love suggests that you don't have a choice and that it's 'destiny'. However, falling in love is about putting someone above you and saying that they are better than you; this is infatuation. Any time you feel yourself falling in love and you have that big high, you are actually saying: *This person is better than me and that is why I feel such a high from being able to attract them.* Yet, even when you get this person attracted to you and are able to get into a relationship with them, if you don't love yourself, this 'love' turns into fear—fear that they are going to leave you for someone else. Then the jealousy and the need to control that person kick in because you don't truly value yourself or really believe that you are worthy of the relationship. Once this fear starts to creep in, it begins to unravel your relationship.

I once worked with a woman who said to me, "I have a checklist; I have a list for my ideal man", and she went through the points such as attractive, intelligent, knows where he's going in life, has a good job, going to make a good father and so on.

I said to her, "That sounds like a really wonderful man. What if you actually had this man in your life and you attracted him? What would you do?" She seemed to have never considered this before because she then looked a bit shocked and said, "I think I'd be a bit afraid actually. In fact, I'd freak out. I'd be so scared of losing him." So I said to her, "Now you can see then, that until you learn to love yourself, attracting people is not the hard part. It's keeping them because if you don't value yourself, you are going to be getting rid of them and will actually be running away from your relationships because you feel you are not worthy of them".

Consider these two options: Would you rather be with somebody who needs you to give them attention all the time in order for them to feel good about themselves or would you rather be with somebody who is very comfortable in their own skin, doesn't make any drama and isn't completely dependent on your attention to make them happy since they are already happy and at peace with who they are? Can you see that each relationship would have a completely different energy? In the latter, you would learn to accept each other for who you are and just allow the peace to pervade your relationship.

Love is unconditional. There is no other love. The only other version that people know is dependency, which is not love. When you depend on someone to make you happy, that's not love. Love is unconditional. Anything else is a cheap substitute. When you learn to love yourself, it is as though your cup is always full and you are ready to pour it out and share this love with as many people as you can. When you don't love yourself, it is as though your cup is always empty and you are desperately searching for somebody to fill it for you.

One of the greatest benefits of learning to love yourself is that you will truly experience unconditional love for yourself and for your partner. When your partner can sense that you love yourself unconditionally, they will feel as though they are loved unconditionally as well. You will start to realise that many of the things you may dislike about them are also within you, thus, you will come to accept these traits in both yourself and your partner.

The ancient oracle at Delphi states, "Know thyself; be thyself; love thyself". This is all about knowing who you are and loving who you are so that you can be truly you. When you can be truly you, you are essentially eliminating your competition. You are the only person that has been made like you. Anytime you are trying to be someone you are not, you are in competition.

If you are a parent, you are going to be a much more peaceful, placid parent who knows just what to do for your children. Every decision you make, even your discipline, will come with an explanation. You will never be motivated to discipline out of frustration or anger but will rather say and do things out of a pure and unconditional love for your child. Because you love yourself, you won't be unconsciously trying to make other people wrong so that you can be right. Love and peace will simply emanate from you. Most of all, you will be the ultimate role model for your children as you teach them the most important thing they can do is learn to love themselves.

Taking Action

Make your list with four columns titled, *Physical, Personality, Good At,* and *Grateful For,* and write as many things under each category as you can. Don't stop until you have at least fifty in each. Put it into your phone or tablet with a daily reminder to read it every morning and night, otherwise you could do it the old-fashioned way and simply post it next to your bed or somewhere you will see it every day; read it once in the morning and once at night.

If there is an activity that you do regularly as an exercise or you have a daily commute, you can mentally go over your list in your head during this time every day. I go over my list while I swim my daily laps at the pool. The point is you don't have to make a huge chunk of time for it. It doesn't take too long and doesn't require a huge effort. The most important thing is that you remember to do it every day in the morning and at night.

Look yourself in the eyes in the mirror once a day and repeat, "I love you", "I love [your name]", and finally, "I love me", three times each.

You could put together a playlist of songs that remind you to love yourself. *Perfect* by P!nk and *Beautiful* by Christina Aguillera are a couple examples. Of course, choose songs that suit your taste and that you enjoy listening to. You don't have to make this playlist all at once. Think of it as an on-going list that you can always add to as you find songs that remind you to love yourself. Listen to your playlist regularly to remind you that you are beautiful, you are perfect, you are not broken and you don't need fixing.

~ *Chapter Seven* ~

KEY NUMBER TWO: READ THE SUBTITLES

Nobody can hurt me without my permission. ~ Mahatma Gandhi

One day, while I was in the playground at one of the schools I taught at, I saw a boy having a go at another kid. I could see the one on the receiving end was feeling hurt and trying to defend himself from the verbal abuse so I walked over to him and said, "You just need to read the subtitles!" Of course, he gave me a look that said *"You must be on drugs, mister. What on earth are you talking about?"* So I elaborated for him, "I heard what this boy called you but the subtitles that were flashing across his chest were, 'I don't like myself. I don't like my life. I need to make you look smaller so that I can look bigger.'"

The five-year-old ego in us loves to say and do things to try and make others appear smaller so that it can appear bigger. I'm sure there have been many times when you got upset or offended by what somebody said or did. However, I'm going to prove that it's not what people say or do that offends you.

Take the example of a mentally ill person who is on medication to keep them stable. They pass by you on the street and swear at you then keep walking. When I pose this scenario to people and ask, "Would you be offended?" They reply, "No, of course not. The person was mentally ill. It had nothing to do with me." So you can see that it's not what people say that hurts you; whether you take offense or not depends on how great a value you place on their words.

By reading the subtitles, you start to realise that every person on this planet wants to feel better about themselves but the five-year-old ego in us doesn't know any other way to achieve this than to put other people down to make them look smaller so that we can look bigger. Someone who wants to own the tallest building in a city could put the time, planning, preparation and energy into building a structure that rises higher than all others around it. The only other option would be to demolish all the other buildings around it until their structure was the highest in the city.

Likewise, you can grow yourself 'tall' through self-love, patience and nurturing, or you can go around 'chopping' others down until you are the biggest building on the block. This is what the ego does because it doesn't know any better way. It is like a five-year-old that will never truly mature. Once you understand this, you will stop taking things personally whenever somebody says or does something with the intention of being offensive because you can spot the ego at work in their actions and understand why it is doing what it does.

The day I realised this, life got a whole lot easier for me. I finally understood a famous quote that I had heard often but never truly understood: "Nobody can hurt me without my permission."

Pain is inevitable. When somebody punches you in the arm, you are going to feel pain. However, the suffering is optional. The suffering would sound something like this: *I can't believe that person punched me. Why did they punch me? They are so horrible.* And the story goes on. The drama continues.

Reading the subtitles means you don't play out anymore stories. No more drama. You are no longer a victim. Unless you learn to read the subtitles, you are going to go on an emotional rollercoaster for the rest of your life and other people are going to be your puppet masters. They'll pull the strings whichever way they like and you will move accordingly. Unless you want to be a puppet, there's a very simple way to cut the strings and that is to *read the subtitles.*

The Buddha, who lived over two thousand years ago, had developed a reputation for being extraordinarily calm and peaceful. One day, a certain man heard about this but he wasn't convinced. He wanted to test the Buddha to see if he could push his buttons. So he went to visit the Buddha and spent some time in his company. For three days, every time the Buddha spoke, this man would have a go at him, picking apart everything he said and trying to discredit him. Every time, the Buddha would simply respond with love and peace. After the third day, the man became tired of this and finally said, "Buddha, how do you stay so calm?" The Buddha replied, "If somebody comes to you with a gift and you do not accept it, to whom does the gift belong?"

What the Buddha was referring to is the gift of hatred. When somebody comes to you with the gift of hatred by trying to push your buttons, just realise that you have the option to reject it and they will be left still holding the gift: their anger.

There was a particular girl who was being bullied at school by being called plenty of unpleasant names. After I coached her, whenever the other kids tried to push her buttons or say things to offend her, she would simply reply with, "Thanks for sharing" and keeps walking or she would simply ignore them altogether. I've worked with kids as young as eight years old to respond in a similar manner. Very soon after, other children stopped bullying this girl because they realised that they weren't getting what they wanted from her. Can you see that it would be pretty silly for somebody to keep trying to push buttons that just weren't there? Eventually they would turn their attention to other people who would allow their strings to be pulled.

Simply responding with, "Is everything alright? Is there something I can do to help?" will leave your offenders rather stumped. They may say, "Did you hear what I just called you?" to which you could just calmly reply, "Yeah, I heard but it sounds like you are having a bad day and if there's anything I can do to help, just let me know." This will leave them speechless; they didn't expect you to respond with love and peace. I think you will find after a while, they will leave you alone because they realise that there are no more buttons to be pushed on you since you would have deactivated them all.

The sporting field spawns countless examples of this. There are always some players who take the bait when they get sledged and they react in outrage, which results in more drama, penalties and angry players on both sides. Then, once in a while, you can find the other type of player who reacts calmly or not at all when the opposition has a go at him; their insults slide like water off a duck's back and the offender realises he just wasted his breath.

I remember one particular summer when the Indian cricket team was playing in Australia. Our Australian team, as they usually do, tried to use verbal intimidation to get on top of their opponents. However, after the game, the general consensus from the Australian players was that it had looked as though their opponents had been *meditating* while they were batting! The Indian batsmen had made a conscious decision to read the subtitles. They took the verbal insults as a sign which says: *We don't think we're good enough so we need to try and cut you guys down to let us get on top.*

When it comes to sport in the public arena, there are always going to be those who resort to verbal abuse to make themselves feel better. However, you always have the ability to choose to see the five-year-old inside others and to realise that they just want what you want, which is to feel better about themselves. Sometimes they resort to letting their ego take lead because they don't know any other way. All they know how to do is to try and make other people feel less so they can seem more. Once you realise that, you will have compassion for them, not anger.

Next time, as soon as somebody says something to you that you would normally be offended by, just take a couple of conscious breaths. Breathe in, breathe out, and just see the five-year-old in yourself and in the other person. Read the subtitles; realise that the message they are actually sending is that they feel smaller than you and are trying to cut you down to bring you to their level. Realise that it's not about you. Don't let this person control your emotions. They won't be able to if you don't allow them to.

When you respond with love and peace, you can quickly be on your way. You will quickly find that there will be fewer people trying to push your buttons because you will be sending out a signal that says *"You can't hurt me; my emotions are beyond your control; you don't control me."* Nobody is going to be able to make you feel anything that you don't want to feel.

Another thing that you can do is to observe interactions between other people. Observe someone having a go at another person. Take notice of when some people just don't seem to react; they stay calm and it doesn't bother them. Then notice other times when people go straight off the end and retaliate. See how it's always a choice and that the same offensive words said to one person could be said to another but the reaction is completely different. The words themselves don't always hurt you. Whether or not you are affected by them depends on whether or not you can read the subtitles.

When you start to read the subtitles, you will become a master of your emotions. You will be able to manage your emotions very well. It's very hard to accomplish any great things in life if you can't manage your emotions. Warren Buffet, the billionaire said, "If you can't manage your emotions, forget about trying to manage money".

The thing I learn as I get older is that no matter what anybody calls you, it's true. This is because there is no human trait that you don't have, which I will talk more about later. However, just understand that whatever anybody calls you, it's fine. There's some truth to it. There may not be any truth to it at that particular moment in time but just know that there's nothing anybody can call you that is untrue in some way.

For example, if somebody says to me, "John, you are so arrogant and self-centred!" I'd reply, "You know what? You might be right. I think there's some truth to that" because I know that if somebody tells me I am mean—well, there have been times when I have been mean but there have also been times that I have been nice.

When you don't get offended by what people say, the purpose for them saying it has lost its power, and because of that, they no longer come back to hound you.

Reading the subtitles will affect all seven areas of your life and will greatly improve the quality of your relationships as it will help you to remove drama from your life and the lives of those around you. It is also particularly important in the field of business and money. If you can stay calm and not react to people, you will be acting from a calm place, which will allow you to perform better in your work and to make wise decisions concerning money.

Taking Action

Practise taking a few deep breaths every time somebody says something that would normally offend you. Notice the ego trying to come up to the surface, ready to defend you. Have a smile, let it go, and just see the five-year-old in the other person wanting to make them feel better. You will be able to relax when you realise that the situation isn't necessarily about you, that it's nothing personal.

Observe other people and their interactions. Notice when some people stay calm even in the face of abuse and notice those who react. Remember that it always comes down to a choice. Notice peaceful people who love themselves and remain calm. Notice how they have no need to put other people down or retaliate when somebody tries to put them down. Anybody who tries to put you down is waving a flag saying *"I don't like myself. I don't like my life. I need to make you look smaller so I look bigger."*

Previously, when somebody said something offensive to you, you might be thrown off-balance, mentally and emotionally. However, by reading the subtitles, you will be getting yourself back into a balanced state and will be able to maintain that calmness and peace from day to day.

~ *Chapter Eight* ~

KEY NUMBER THREE: OBSERVE YOUR THOUGHTS

*The highest form of human intelligence is to observe yourself
without judgement. ~ Jiddu Krishnamurti*

We have established that it is not what people say that offends us; it is whether we put a value on what people say.

So what does offend you? What bothers you? Why do you feel pain? It simply comes down to not observing your thoughts. You feed your thoughts with emotions. We often allow thoughts to sit in our head and we feed them, giving them emotions. Unless you observe your thoughts and learn to let go of unimportant ones, you are going to be a slave to them. When those thoughts are unpleasant, they will be able to make you feel some pretty unpleasant things every time they go through your mind because you are not mastering them.

It's very hard to focus on the task at hand or develop quality relationships if you are stuck in your head and you can't get a thought out of your mind. If you don't observe your thoughts, you become a sleepwalker, somebody who gets lost in their thoughts to the point where they are oblivious to the world and life passes you by.

It's been estimated that the average adult human has 60,000 separate thoughts each day and it has been found that over 95% of those thoughts are the same ones from the previous day. The point is, we have lots of thoughts that don't mean much of anything at all and most of them are the same ones we had yesterday. So when a thought pops into your head and you feed it a particular emotion such as hurt, anger or frustration, it's going to come back knocking on your door again like a beggar asking you for more food. However, if it keeps coming back and you say, "Sorry, not today!" it might come back a couple days later and if you turn it away again, eventually it will get the message that it's not going to be fed and will stop coming back to bother you.

When you fuel a thought with emotional energy, it will keep coming back. But if you observe it, simply let it pass or throw it out like a piece of rubbish, have a laugh at it and realise it doesn't mean anything, pretty soon it stops coming back. It's either replaced by a positive thought or even better, no thought at all. You will be left with a calm, clean mind, free from distractions or unnecessary worry.

Human beings are quite intuitive in that it's not really other people that hurt us but rather, our own minds. Evidence of this is can be found when taking a look at the many addictions of society.

Alcohol suppresses one's thoughts; it slows them down; it hits the pause button. Many men will say they feel more confident after having a few drinks. What they're really saying is: *If I drink enough, then the thoughts that tell me I'm not good enough seem to subside and allow me to be more confident.* However, that comes with a heavy price.

Drugs will also suppress and muddle your thoughts. So too with excessive TV-watching, internet and social media addiction. This is one reason for many people becoming so absorbed with their phones and other technology. These are a constant distraction from what is really going on in their mind.

Philosopher Blaise Pascal once said, "All man's misery derives from not being able to sit quietly in a room alone". This is why we feel the need to be distracted and not take time to be on our own, to simply enjoy our own company. Most people are afraid of what their own mind tells them.

The need to suppress thoughts has become a multi-trillion-dollar industry. Not only are a lot of businesses servicing these addictions feeding them so that the cycle continues endlessly, they also sell medications to help prevent symptoms of anxiety caused by excessive thoughts going through people's minds.

But there *is* a way to end the cycle permanently.

Once you realise that you can observe your thoughts, watch them and allow them to pass, you will find there's a sense of peace that comes from knowing that you are in control of whether a thought bothers you or not. The thoughts themselves have no energy to them. It's whether you feed them that determines how often they will return to trouble you.

When I introduce some people to the concept of observing your thoughts, they get a little bit freaked out when I mention this next bit: There are really two in each of us. Or you could say that we are divided into two parts. I'm not talking about two separate personalities but indeed, two very different persons. Eckhart Tolle once stated, "When people say, 'I am angry with myself', can you see which one is upset with the other? So which one am I?"

I ask you to do this now: Sit quietly for about thirty seconds and just observe the next thought that pops into your mind. Don't judge it; just observe it. Can you see that you tapped into the *observer*, the *watcher*, the *consciousness*, the *awareness*? Whatever names given to it—that's the invisible part of you. If you didn't have that part of you, you wouldn't even know you were thinking. You would just be thinking without knowing you were thinking. In doing this exercise, you were able to observe the *thinker*, the *ego*, the mind that always gives random thoughts—it's a reflex organ. You cannot stop your thoughts but you can observe them and allow them to pass.

If you sat all day in a room with bare walls, no pictures, no music, no furniture, no stimulus whatsoever, you would realise that you still have thoughts. Even without any external stimulus, your mind would go on thinking, throwing thoughts at you. So the thoughts just happen but the energy you give to thoughts, fuelling them to continue, is optional.

Now that you know the nature of the ego, you realise that the ego wants you to feel like a victim by hanging onto the thoughts that say you are not good enough because these will get your attention. However, when you love yourself and you are reading the subtitles, you realise that you don't need to feed the thoughts any emotion. You don't need to become a victim to get love and attention since you already have it.

One thing that you might want to do once or twice a week is to sit down for ten minutes and simply write down any thought that pops into your head during this time, regardless of what it is. Don't judge it; just observe it and write it down. You are going to find some pretty random things, some repetitive stuff and some of it may make you laugh. Some of it will make you shake your head but don't judge it. Just have a laugh and let it pass. Just observe and watch how most of the thoughts you have day to day are pretty repetitive and don't mean much of anything at all.

In your day-to-day life, anytime you feel any negative emotion, just stop and notice that you are not feeling good and ask yourself this one question: *What thought is going through my head right now?* Then observe the thought; don't judge it. Just observe it and allow it to pass.

The inability to observe your thoughts is the reason why some people look lost in their mind or 'space out' when you are speaking to them sometimes; they may appear very distracted and you question whether they have actually listened to what you said. Now if you are honest with yourself, you will probably realise that there are times when you do this exact same thing while other people are talking to you.

When you are able to observe your thoughts and allow them to pass, the quality of your relationships will improve. People will really feel that you are listening when they speak to you and they will appreciate this.

When I was younger, I used to suffer from insomnia. I've overcome that through being able to observe my thoughts and just allow them to pass. When you really cannot fall sleep, I truly believe that 99% of the time it's due to the thought that keeps playing through your mind and when you keep feeding them, they continue on and on. Your brain thinks you need to stay awake to keep feeding the thoughts. Once you learn to allow the thoughts to pass, you fall into a lovely cycle of sleep. I haven't had any problems sleeping for the last five years since teaching myself to simply 'step back' and observe my thoughts.

If you don't observe your thoughts, an endless cycle of trying to replace bad thoughts with better ones will perpetuate. It's a lot of effort to try and replace negative thoughts with positive thoughts. It's so much easier to just watch them and allow them to pass. But if you keep reading your list of what you love about yourself and what you are grateful for, teach yourself to read the subtitles and practise observing your thoughts, you are going to find a natural decline in the volume of thoughts that go through your head that simply don't serve you.

If you are somebody who has trouble sleeping, when you go to bed, just concentrate on your breathing. Grab any thought that passes through your head like it's a piece of paper, scrunch it up, throw it away and just allow it to gently float past you down the river.

When you are able to observe your thoughts, you will find yourself less distracted and be able to focus much better. This is going to increase the quality of your work, study, family and social life.

When you start to observe your thoughts, you will no longer turn to addictions such as drugs, alcohol, gambling, excessive TV-watching, internet and social media addiction, etc.

When you love yourself, read the subtitles and can observe your thoughts, you will find that you will feel less of a pull towards those addictions because you don't feel the need to press the pause button on your mind or run away from your thoughts. You will know that at any time you can just watch the thoughts and let them go.

Think about how much money you will save by being free of certain addictions—think of all the money that you will be able to put to a better use such as building a business, providing a better life for your family and most importantly, rewarding yourself for the new place of peace you have found.

Taking Action

A couple of times a week or every day if you have time, sit and write down any thought that pops into your mind for two minutes. Don't judge anything; just write them down. Some of the thoughts may startle, confuse or even humour you. Just laugh them off; allow them to pass. You will realise a lot of your thoughts don't mean much of anything and that they're pretty repetitive.

Notice any time you have a negative emotion; stop, take a couple of breaths and ask yourself, *What thought is going through my head right now?* Simply observe it. If it doesn't serve you, throw it out like it's a piece of trash. It doesn't mean anything. Do not feed it. Otherwise, it will keep coming back.

~ *Chapter Nine* ~

KEY NUMBER FOUR:
BE PRESENT

Realize deeply that the present moment is all you ever have" ~ Eckhart Tolle

Do you ever stop and wonder at the wonderful gift we have been given that is the miracle of life? Yet, most people spend their lifetime thinking about what happened in the past or what needs to happen in the future before they can be happy. Do you realise that anytime your mind is in the past or in the future, you are not actually really living; you are just sleepwalking? Too many people let this precious gift of life pass them by because they're stuck in a memory or they're anticipating a fantasy that doesn't exist and may never come true. Unless you are living fully present in the moment, each moment of every day, your life is literally passing you by.

I was guilty of this when I was younger. My mind would be stuck in the past or dreaming of what my life needed to become before I could be happy. Meanwhile, I would zone in and out through my day-to-day life. My concentration wasn't there; I wasn't really listening to people when they spoke to me because I wasn't present for them.

When you think about it, you will realise the present moment is all you ever have. Five minutes from now will be now. Five hours from now will be now. When has your life ever been anything but *now*?

I ask myself three questions to help to keep me present. The first question is: *Where are you?* The answer is: *Here.* Wherever you are is *here*, no matter what the name of the place is, it's always *here.*

The second question is: *What time is it?* The answer is always *now.* When has your life ever been anything but *now*? There is no past, there is no future; there truly is just one eternal *now.*

Finally: *What are you?* The answer is the present moment, *this moment.* You realise that you are not the person you were five years ago, five weeks ago, not even five days ago. You are always where you are and who you are in *this present moment.* That's all you ever are, all you ever will be.

When you begin your action steps towards this Key, something you may find helpful for the first week is to put a reminder in your phone that alerts you every few hours, prompting you to read it. All it has to say is: *Here. Now. This moment.*

As you go about your day-to-day activities, choose a couple of tasks that you normally do and do them differently now by giving them your full attention. For an example, while you are washing your hands, notice the feel and sound of the water; notice the smell of the soap; let yourself get lost in the activity by just being totally devoted to the experience you are having in that moment without thinking about anything else.

When you start to be present, you really make your life all about the journey and not the destination. You are not thinking too far ahead but appreciating . . . *This might be the only moment I'll ever have so I'm going to live it and appreciate it.*

With practising being present comes gratitude. You will start to realise that, *I don't need anything in particular to happen for me to be happy. I can just be happy within this moment and give it my full attention,* and because you are being present, your ego goes to sleep and you can fully relax.

The ego, by nature, needs to have predictability because it equates predictability with a greater success or survival rate. Wouldn't you agree that if you could predict what was going to happen next week or next year, you would feel a lot safer? Unfortunately, as human beings, we're not created with the innate ability to tell the future (at least I know I wasn't), so predicting the events of tomorrow or next year is essentially impossible.

Think about a time in the past when you changed schools or jobs or relocated to a different house. There was probably some anxiety involved in that move because the ego didn't know what was going to happen and needed time to realise that the change was safe. To your ego, the change was not safe but remember that you can remind your ego that change is safe; it's totally fine; in fact, it is a natural and beneficial part of life.

Because it wants predictability, the ego keeps looking out for a pattern, so when you are being present, the ego says: *Well, I see that you are fully present right now.* And anyone who is fully present is as safe as they're going to be. So the ego says: *I guess you are safe right now since you are fully present, living right in the moment, so nothing is a threat to you.*

The more you practise being present, the more you practise putting your ego to sleep; you will be taking over the driver's seat, which is where you belong, and letting the five-year-old ego ride in the passenger's seat where it belongs. Now you are driving, you are in charge and the ego's fallen asleep; it's quiet and not disrupting you. It may wake up occasionally and you will hear it but you don't need to give it attention; you don't need to feed it.

If a five-year-old came up to you on the street and told you how terrible you were, would you really talk back to it to try and defend yourself? Just see that is all your ego is, a five-year-old. Laugh and smile; know it's there and just let it talk without responding. Don't give it attention and it will fall right back to sleep.

So during your week, practise being present in all areas of your life. Practise it spiritually: If you are reading a book, really give it your attention. Or if you are listening to someone give a talk, really be there. Practise being present in your work. Watch how the quality of your work improves and how the rewards will come to you through finances and promotions, etc. Practise being present in your relationships with your friends and your family. Be a conscious listener; notice how they feel more loved when you are really there for them and how much love they will want to show give you in return. Sometimes people will question whether you truly love them and want to be with them if your mind is elsewhere. Practising being present allows not only your relationships to improve but the quality of your life overall because you get to share in some wonderful moments with other people and really be there to experience and remember them.

When you are living in the present, you will begin to notice the signs around you, the guidance from God and the universe, the source of life. You will start to be aware of them. You will realise that they were always there before but you simply weren't watching for them and so you may have never noticed them until now.

Before I found peace and was able to be present, it was as if I was driving on a motorway and there were billboards and signs pointing me in the right direction towards my destination, all giving me clues and hints; but because I was so lost in my own mind, in the past or in the future, I didn't notice them. People said to me, "Didn't you see those signs?" and I replied, "What signs?" When I became present, I started to notice all these signs around me, guiding me.

There's a great scene from the film *Bruce Almighty* which illustrates this perfectly. The main character is driving his car down the road and pleading for God to give him a sign while there are signs literally all around him and in front of him, but because he's not present and he's lost in his own mind, he doesn't see them. Eventually he has an accident, which wakes him up to all the signs that were around him the whole time, pointing him in the right direction.

The reason why so many people love extreme sports like skydiving, snowboarding or surfing is because it forces the participant to be present while engaging in the activity. When I went skydiving four years ago, the one thing that I realised while I was falling was that I had such an adrenaline rush because I wasn't thinking about what happened in the past; I wasn't thinking about anything I had to do tomorrow; I was 100% totally devoted to the experience I was having; I was happy living entirely in the moment. It was blissful.

Whenever you do something dangerous that involves a great amount of risk, you are required to give the activity your full and undivided attention. You are forced to be present as you focus on the moment because your body wants to keep you alive. This is what extreme sports enthusiasts get addicted to. They love the fact that their mind has switched off, that they're not thinking about anything else besides, *I need to focus fully on this task in order to stay alive.*

This is why many people, even seemingly hard-hearted people, love to be around children, especially new-borns and infants. Children remind us that being present is really all about the wonder of life and stopping to realise, *You know what? This is awesome. Just look at how wonderful life is!*

I believe that apart from seeing the beauty and the innocence of a little child, most people love holding little children and looking after them because it forces them into the present moment. They can't be thinking about the past or the future. It requires their full attention and with that comes a pausing of the thoughts and relief from the mind's games.

When you start practising being present, look out for the signs that will sometimes appear out of nowhere. Realise that you are constantly being guided by a higher source, by a loving energy and that you are not alone. The more you practise being present, the more you will know God; the more you will realise that you have been guided your whole life and that there have been signs for you through your whole life though you may only be beginning to notice them now.

The signs tend to come in threes. The first one may raise an eyebrow. By the time the second one comes, you will begin to wonder, *Is this a coincidence?* But once the third one hits you, it'll be like a knockout punch; it will leave you in no doubt.

This happened to me when I had to decide where I would go to teach overseas. Initially, my plan was to go to London, as many Australians do, to teach and travel around Europe. However, life threw me a spinner in the works. I wasn't able to go to London at the time I had planned due to having to finish a couple of subjects later than expected. That same year, I briefly dated a woman who was also a teacher. While we were together, she asked me, "Have you thought about teaching in South Korea?" My reaction was something like, "South Korea? No, I've never thought of that. Thanks though", and I sort of shoved the suggestion up into the attic of my brain. She explained to me how she had gone and really enjoyed it but I just said, "Well, my plan was to go to London and travel around Europe. I feel like I'm meant to go to Europe".

About a month or so later, I met a teacher who had done both, taught in London and taught in South Korea. She raved about South Korea, how wonderful the kids were, how respectful they were and what a wonderful experience it had been getting to know a new culture. She also told me about her experiences teaching in London and basically said that if she didn't have a fight in a class, it was considered a good class.

When I heard this I thought, *This is weird; it must be a coincidence. I've heard about South Korea twice now in the space of a couple months.*

But it was the third sign that really got my attention.

I had booked a flight to go with my brother to the Gold Coast in July that year. Several days before we left, my brother said to me, "John, I want you to change the flights. Can we go on the earliest flight there and the latest one back?" This was fine with me so I made last-minute rearrangements to our flights.

A couple weeks later, we were on our flight back from the Gold Coast on a Thursday night; it was nearly 10 o'clock and I remember sitting down with my brother after boarding the plane. My brother was in the window seat, I had the middle seat and there was one empty seat left next to us. As the passengers finished boarding, a man who looked to be about my age walked past our aisle and then came back a moment later to ask if he could sit in the seat next to me.

He told me an amazing story. He said he wasn't even supposed to be on this flight. Work had sent him up to the Gold Coast for a seminar but he had slept in and missed his flight home. He also told me how he was in a lot of debt and that he didn't have the money to book another ticket so he called his boss in Aubrey and said, "Look, I'm going to hitchhike back to Sydney and get a lift from Sydney to Aubrey". So he tried hitchhiking and a car pulled over for him. The driver was a middle-aged man who was a doctor. He explained to the driver what had happened and the doctor replied to him, "My wife and I are about to have dinner. How about you come back to our place, have some dinner with us, and I'll pay for a ticket home for you".

And so there he was sitting in the seat next to me just a few hours later. I was amazed by his story and I couldn't help thinking, *He wasn't even supposed to be on this flight and neither was I.* But here is where the amazing thing really happened.

We began talking about our careers and what we each did. I explained I was a teacher and he said he was an engineer. Then we got around to talking about family and I asked him, "Do you have any siblings?" He said that he had a twin brother. My next question was, "What does your brother do for work?" and he replied, "Well, my brother left for South Korea three weeks ago to teach English".

My jaw dropped. I turned to my brother who I swear mouthed the words, "What the fudge!"

That was the third and most powerful sign. I realised then and there that I was being guided. I was fully present so I had been able to see the signs and take them to heart.

I went to South Korea, not fully knowing why, only trusting that I needed to be there. That year in South Korea, I grew as a person and as a teacher. I got out of my comfort zone. I immersed myself in a culture I knew very little about and embraced the experience. I learned to be adaptable. It was a life-changing experience and I will forever be glad I followed the signs I was given and made the decision to go.

My point is that if you are not present, you can miss the signs. You don't really notice them or they seem too subtle for you to take them to heart and to act upon them, so you let them slip by you without giving them any further thought.

If you think there is something special about me, there isn't. You are getting the signs too. Perhaps you simply have not been present enough to notice them. So start to be present, look for the signs and you will realise you are being guided. Whether it's toward a certain career or to do with travelling, whether it's concerning a relationship—just notice that there are always signs being given to you all over the place. Once you are present, you will notice them. Remember, they often will come in threes and will grab your attention.

If you don't learn to be present, life is going to pass you by and one day you are going to ask yourself, *What happened to my life?* because you won't remember half of what you did. There will be less quality in all areas of your life. However, the more you practise being present, the greater the overall quality of your life and your relationships will be, and with that comes the abundance.

When my son was three years old, I asked him the questions, "Where are you? What time is it? What are you?" He learned it in the first go. I asked him again the next day and his answers were, "Here. Now. This moment".

If you have children, it's important to teach them from a young age to be present. Ask them the questions. Get them to be fully present and really appreciate that the only time they will ever have is now and everything else is not guaranteed; everything else is either a memory or a future anticipation. It does not exist in the real world.

By being in the present moment, you will really start to enjoy the process of things and not focus on the result. This greatly helps children especially when it comes to academics. Getting them to fall in love with the present moment and not worry so much about the result will allow them to enjoy the process, which will be much more likely to give them the result they want in the end anyway.

Same as on the sporting field. When you can be fully present in the moment and not get attached to a result by simply focussed on the here and now, you will really enjoy the process of playing, which is what you are spending so much time and energy on anyway. But just watch how the quality of your performance will improve.

Same too with performing in drama or music. When you are fully present, the quality of your work just increases. The greatest obstacle for your being present is thoughts you don't observe. So observe your thoughts and then throw them out. Remember, anything that prevents you from being in the here and now is trash. Throw it out if it does not serve you. Keep your mind clear and you will be able to truly focus and enjoy life in the present moment.

Taking Action

Choose any task that you do on a regular day-to-day basis and just practise giving it your full attention. Whether it's washing dishes, playing a game, speaking or listening to somebody—whatever it is, just make that your 'be-present' task that you give your 100% full attention. Notice how there's an absence of drama when you do this; there's an absence of the ego. You will feel calmness and peaceful. Practise it daily.

Perhaps put a reminder in your phone prompting you daily with the three questions: *Where are you? What time is it? What are you?* followed by the answers: *Here. Now. This moment.*

Start to look for signs. Ask yourself, *What is the question I would like answered? Does it have to do with work or finances or a relationship?* and then just practise looking out for the signs. Wait for the signs to come and be present. They will come and when they do, you will be able to see them and you will realise that you are being guided; you've never been alone.

A wonderful book that talks a lot more about how to be present is *The Power of Now* by Eckhart Tolle. It really delves a lot deeper into the concept of being present and how to stay present throughout your everyday life. Check it out when you get a chance. You won't regret it.

~ Chapter Ten ~

KEY NUMBER FIVE: THERE IS NO GOOD OR BAD

Remember, for everything you have lost, you have gained something else.
Without the dark, you would never see the stars. ~ David Wolfe

Labelling things as 'good' or 'bad' is yet another way to continue riding through life on a rollercoaster. When things are seemingly 'good', you get to ride on a high but when things are 'bad', you will be in a low. There is nothing balanced about a rollercoaster ride. It is neither a happy nor healthy way to live one's life and truly experience abundance.

According to William Shakespeare, "Nothing is ever good or bad. Only your thinking makes it so", and there is a lot of truth to that.

I use my own story as an example of this. When I am teaching or coaching, I tell people about some of the things that I went through when I was younger. I tell them about how I went to TAFE and enrolled in a course I despised but then realised I wanted to go back and do my HSC (Higher School Certificate) for the second time. I then ask them, "Was that good or bad?" and they say, "Well, I think that's good". I describe how I went on from there to do really well in my HSC and was able to get into the degree I wanted. "Was that good or bad?" Most people say, "That was good".

The story continues: I'm nearing the completion of my degree and I happen to meet a sports manager and agent who tells me exactly what her job is like and what she has to do. Something inside me just shrivels up and says, *That's not me at all. I can't see myself doing that,* and I decide I'm going to have to change my choice of direction in career. When I ask people, "Was that good or bad?" Generally, they say, "Well, that was bad".

From there, my life spirals into depression and I hit rock bottom. I think about committing suicide. Most people would say that's pretty bad. After hitting rock bottom, I choose to seek help and I come out of my depression, realising that I feel I am meant to be a teacher. Is that good or bad?

After being a teacher for a couple of years, my relationship with my fiancé breaks down. Good or bad? From the breakdown of that relationship, I decide to travel overseas and experience a new culture. I end up going to teach in South Korea for a year. The year changes me personally and professionally and is one of the most rewarding experiences of my life. Obviously, most people say, "That's great!"

After living more than a year overseas, I come back and I meet a beautiful woman whom I fall in love with and we get married. People say, "Well, that's good." But hardly a year later, I realise I've made a huge mistake and I've married for the wrong reasons. People usually say this was bad.

After deciding to be single for a while, I meet a wonderful partner who supports me in my goals and values, is very calm and loves who she is. People always say this must have been really good.

From there, I really discover inner peace and start to practise the principles I'm teaching and through that, I branch out in my work and start motivational speaking, helping young people, teaching them about how to be at peace. Most importantly, I am able to relate to them because I was in a dark place myself at one point. The same goes for my life coaching. I'm able to help more adults because of what I've been through and thus, my ability to relate to them.

Can you see that nothing that has happened in my life is either good or bad? All those experiences have simply been steps in the journey to where I am today. I needed all those experiences, every part of that journey, to be able to be where I am today. There was no good or bad. I was never a victim. It was just all part of my training for a bigger purpose in life.

It can be hard to see it at first but when you stand back and just ask yourself: *How is what I'm experiencing helping me to fulfil what I value most? How is what I'm experiencing allowing me to grow as a person?* you will begin to realise that everything happens for a reason.

The same principle goes for personality traits. There are things in myself I used to label as bad and tried to label in other people as bad, until I realised that nothing I do is bad. Everything has a purpose.

I was fortunate enough to attend a workshop with Dr Demartini where I learned a process that allowed me to see the perfection to how things are. I strongly recommend you to look into attending the same workshop by Dr Demartini if you ever get the chance. It is called '*The Breakthrough Experience*' and truly is just that. It is liberating to realise that nothing is bad; everything has a purpose. When you can realise that, you will see the divinity in everything. You will know God and understand his divine purpose for your life. You will realise that nothing is chaotic but rather, everything has an order to it.

Let us look at how to balance or neutralise your perceptions of other people based on Dr Demartini's method.

Think of a person who really pushes your buttons, the one who is most annoying to you. Now list the traits they possess that annoy you the most. Next, go down the list of traits and for each one, ask yourself this question: *Who in my life has seen me exhibit the exact same trait?* Scan the seven areas of your life—Spiritual, Intellectual, Work, Money, Family, Friends, Health—and look for examples of times when you have exhibited the exact same trait. Own up to it and admit that whatever is in them is also in you.

Next, look at how the person benefitted you from being the way they were in these situations. It may be difficult at first to find the benefits from seemingly bad events. However, when you look closely, you may find that as a result of their trait, you didn't want to spend as much time with them and that forced you into spiritual reflection. Perhaps you decided you were going to research into something that you really love or you focussed on spending more time on your work or with your family. Perhaps you made more money in this extra free time or you just decided you wanted to spend more time with your closest friends because of this and those friendships grew stronger as a result. Maybe you decided to spend more quality time with your partner. Maybe the person's actions helped to teach you patience. Once you start searching for all the positives, you will find them; they are always there.

The next step is to think of examples of when you have seen this person exhibit the opposite of this trait and then acknowledge that there are two sides to this person; nobody is ever one-sided. Everyone has been greedy. Everyone has been generous in some way before. Everyone has been honest and dishonest. Everyone has been kind and been cruel. Once you see both sides, you realise that they are not only one thing but that they are both. Doing the same process with yourself, you start to realise there's no shame and guilt in you possessing this trait either. What I have learned is that whatever you see in somebody else that you don't like is really a part of you that you've tried to disown.

Schopenhauer, the German philosopher, says, "We become our true selves to the degree that we make everybody else ourselves". The only thing in another person that can annoy you is something that you don't think is within you, something that you've disowned. So while you think that these people have been sent to torture or to punish you, believe that they are your greatest teachers. They are holding up a mirror and saying, "This is something you haven't owned up to yet. Isn't it about time you did?"

Once you realise all the benefits that have come out of this person displaying this trait, you look at how people benefitted from you displaying the same trait. Once you balance that out in your mind, you will realise you don't need to feel guilty or ashamed about it.

Next, you look for what you would have lost had they not displayed this trait. What would you have not gained had they not displayed this trait? You realise you would have lost all the benefits we mentioned earlier. When I went through this process myself and when I do it now with my clients, we see the perfection of the trait and that it was neither good nor bad, that something was gained rather than lost. You also start to learn and love the trait that you previously disowned. You have more love for yourself as well as the person that you were frustrated with.

Keep in mind that when you do this process, it's not necessarily about looking for the trait in the exact form. For example, it might be that you are angry with someone who you think is stingy with money. If you are generous with money, just look for times when you've been stingy with money also because you can't be generous unless you have stinginess in you, otherwise you will have no money left to give. Additionally, look for other times when you might have displayed different forms of stinginess such as with your love, praise or affection.

Go through each of the traits that you listed and balance them out in this fashion. By the end of it, not only will you have more compassion for this person, you will also have more love for yourself. It doesn't necessarily mean you are going to want to be best mates and hang out with this person all the time but you will no longer have a charge around these traits. In fact, you will see that they serve a purpose.

I was coaching a woman a few years ago who said to me, "I wish everybody would just get this and be able to live in peace rather than cause drama in the world". I replied, "Well, can you see that the person who you thought was causing you the most drama has led you to life coaching, put you on this path to spiritual reflection and has lead you to find inner peace?" The woman smiled as she then realised that her whole life had led her to this point in time and that there was never such a thing as a good or bad experience. That smile said to me, *Ah, I get it now. I am not a victim; I never was. It's all been part of my journey. It was always meant to be and happened for a reason.*

She also saw that people who unconsciously cause suffering in the world actually help a lot of people to wake up because it's often the pain that wakes you up. It's the pain that makes you look within. It's the pain that helps you look at things clearer.

Once you have balanced out all the traits, you should find that you no longer have any anger towards that person and you just realise that you can say thank you to them for being the way they are. If they weren't that way, you wouldn't have what you have now and you wouldn't be where you are right now.

When this realisation first 'clicked' with me, it gave me a sense of peace because I realised my whole life had played out exactly the way it was meant to, that I was meant to meet people who'd push my buttons so I could learn to love others and myself more. Now whenever I meet somebody who pushes any of my buttons, rather than getting angry with them, I stand back, observe the situation and I own up to the trait in myself. I go through the process and I learn to love that in them so that I can love it in me.

You can also go through a slight variation of the process with yourself and the traits you dislike about yourself. If there is anything in you that you don't like or are ashamed of, go through the process; list them all and find the balance. Look at what you have gained and what you would have missed as well as what others may have missed out on. Ask yourself what you learned from the situations in which you displayed the traits you dislike. What were the possible benefits for those you interacted with? What would have been the negatives, the drawbacks, had you not displayed those traits? You will start to see the perfection dissolves any shame or guilt you have around what you previously perceived to be 'bad'.

Finally, take a look at the events you have labelled as 'bad' in your life. Look at them from a different perspective; step back and observe as though they were playing out on a television screen. Just do a little analysing. Ask yourself: *What did I miss at the time this happened? Can I read the subtitles now? Can I see that people were going through their own drama and it had nothing to do with me?*

Can you see what you learned from and how you learned from it? Can you see something that you missed, something that you didn't realise at the time? And can you see how your life has gone on this journey since then? Maybe the experience led you to a life-changing book or to meeting somebody important. Maybe it led you to counselling. Maybe it led you to look within to do a little crucial self-reflection. Maybe it led you to start your own business. Maybe you even met your life partner as a result. So can you see that there was something to learn from it and that it led you to something else?

Once you view it without emotion, from the point of view of the observer, you will see the balance. You will see that there was never any good or bad—that everything was happening for a reason; to teach you something, to help you grow. God, the universe, the spirit—whatever you would like to call it—wants you to grow and expand your soul. The only way it can get your attention sometimes is to gently tap your shoulder. If that doesn't work then it may have to yank your shirt, then punch your shoulder, then give you a knockout blow—but it will do whatever it takes to get your attention and it is all for your own good. If it doesn't do that, it can't get your attention. If it can't get your attention, it's very hard for you to grow.

One of my students, a fifteen-year-old girl, seemed upset one day while I was teaching a class. Later, I asked her what was upsetting her and she explained that she was angry because her ex-boyfriend was inconsiderate. I asked her if she would be open to doing a process that would help her to get over this frustration quickly and she agreed. I started by asking her, "Who, in your life, has seen you being inconsiderate before?" I helped her scan all the areas of her life with slight prompting and afterwards, she realised family members, friends and classmates had all seen her be inconsiderate before. After a while, she said, "Yep, I've got it just as much as him".

Then we looked for the benefits of her ex-boyfriend being inconsiderate and she realised that through his inconsideration, she had grown closer to her family and friends, saved money and was focussing more on school. Then we looked at how other people had benefitted from her being inconsiderate and we realised there were just as many benefits when she exhibited the trait.

Next, she was able to acknowledge that her ex-boyfriend had the opposite trait in him—he had been considerate as well—and that many people around him had seen him be considerate many times. Additionally, when he was being inconsiderate to her, she realised that family and friends had opportunities to exhibit more consideration towards her, so that in the end nothing was ever missing, she was never really lacking anything; she had the perfect balance all the time.

When we finally looked at what she would have lost had he been anything but inconsiderate, a sense of peace portrayed by a smile spread across her face. That smile said: *I get it; I realise that I'm not a victim. Everything happens for a reason. I just couldn't see it at first.*

Taking Action

Go through the process as I described. Start by listing the traits in others and yourself that you particularly dislike, and then think of times when you have seen the opposite of these traits displayed by yourself or others. Think of all the ways people have benefitted from situations you have previously labelled as 'bad' and think of what may have been missed out on had the situation not panned out so. Perhaps you might want to focus on owning up to one trait a day and do that regularly. Eventually, you will find that you no longer have any anger or resentment towards those in your life whom you have trouble getting along with. Eventually, you will erase any regret or anger you may have at yourself or your past. You will be freed completely and those negative feelings will be replaced by inner peace and calm.

Another thing you can do is to research Dr Demartini. Go to his website; read his books, attend a live workshop of his if you ever get the chance. You will gain greater clarity about the background of this concept and insight on the science of it all, the beauty of how the human brain works and how the process plays out at a neurological level. You will get to know why and how this process will work for you and can work for everyone. I highly recommend you try to attend his workshop, *'The Breakthrough Experience'* one day if you are at all able to. It is truly life-changing and one of the most insightful experiences you may ever have.

Perhaps keep Shakespeare's quote, "There is no good or bad. Only our thinking makes it so", up next to you somewhere in your workspace or bedroom to serve as a simple reminder for you of this on a daily basis.

~ *Chapter Eleven* ~

GOAL-SETTING IN THE SEVEN AREAS OF YOUR LIFE

A goal without a plan is just a wish. ~ Antoine de Saint-Exuperys

It is important to specifically identify your goals anytime you are embarking on any journey towards bettering yourself and your life. By setting goals for yourself, you are outlining a timeline saying, *I want to achieve this by this deadline or within this certain timeframe.* If you don't set a timeline, it really is just a dream, not a goal. When do you have dreams? When you are asleep, not when you are awake and active. By setting goals for yourself, your dreams become tangible; they become realistic. By setting a timeframe within which you would like to achieve your goals, you are affirming your belief in yourself, your belief that you will be able to achieve your goals. If you are unable to set a timeframe for them, this may tells you that you don't believe they are possible and you lack the necessary faith in yourself to reach your goals.

What I recommend you to do is to draw up a simple chart with seven columns which you can title, *Spiritual, Intellectual, Work, Money, Family, Friends* and *Physical.* Now as you go on your journey, you can keep track of your goals by categorising them amongst the seven areas of your life. You may be thinking, *I don't really have any specific goals for each of these areas right now; all I know is that I want inner peace.* The thing is, setting these goals for yourself is one of the most important parts of the process towards achieving peace and balance in your life. What I am saying is that this is a step you do not want to skip. It will help you keep track of the goals you have made and when or whether you have achieved them so that you can look back along the way, gauge your progress and analyse to find the areas where you need to focus on improving the most. It will also give you a clear picture of what it is you want to accomplish by breaking down your large goals into smaller stepping stones, which will help you make the quickest progress.

Even if you did not have any clear and specific goals outlined in your mind when you started out on this journey, do this now. Go through every area of your life, each column and start by thinking of one goal to write under each. Form a clear picture of it in your mind and put it into written words. They do not have to be big goals. They can be as simple and small as you would like. Just be sure they are indeed goals you are motivated to accomplish.

Next, set a timeframe or deadline for each. Make sure you are realistic about this because if you do not give yourself realistic deadlines by which to achieve your goals, you may end up feeling discouraged if you are unable to reach them within your timeframe.

Also set up a schedule for your goals. This is all about breaking down big goals into smaller steps that will help you to best achieve your goals. For an example, under *Spiritual,* you may decide that you want to read through a list of books by the greatest spiritual teachers that have ever lived. Obviously, this is not a goal that will be achieved within a few months or even a few years but you can start with giving yourself structure by deciding on a time and frequency through which you will work towards it. Firstly, it may help if you narrow it down to a list of perhaps twenty-five or fifty books. Then you may decide that every day you would like to set aside an hour for this reading or it may be every other day or twice a week. Perhaps it will be a total of three hours over the weekend to be completed anytime over the two days, but it's best to decide on a specific time during the days you read and try to stick to this schedule. Once you have decided on your schedule, don't forget to put reminders in your phone or tablet to help you stay on track. The habit will help your brain to alert you if you miss a time. Your brain's natural prompting will be to your advantage.

You don't have to try to work towards all your goals at the same time. You could prioritise them and choose to stick with one or two for now until you have completed those and then work on another one or two later on down the track. Although for now, write at least one goal under each column for every area of your life.

Intellectually, it may be that you want to read about a specific industry or research something that you are really interested in that will further your career; you may want to read things that will help you gain knowledge about something specific and to help you become an expert in that particular field. Perhaps you are interested in joining a club or taking classes that will help expand your knowledge and experience in a field of your passion. Again, decide if you want to do this daily, weekly or monthly. Make a decision and then choose the days of the week and a time of the day then schedule it into your personal electronic devices with a reminder.

Next is *Work.* Do you have goals to start your own business? Do you have goals to get a promotion? Are there classes you need to take or certifications you must obtain to gain a promotion? Just set a goal that you would like to accomplish in your work life. It may be that you want to network once a month to meet other people in your industry, possibly find a joint venture or just make valuable connections. It might be that you set a twelve-month goal towards slowly getting out of your current work so that you can do something that you truly love. You could set monthly goals in succession, a step-by-step way of slowly unplugging from what you are currently doing to eventually fully replacing your source of income with doing what you really love.

Next, set your goals when it comes to *Finances.* Do you have a weekly goal of saving 10% that goes straight into your savings account where you won't touch it for now? Do you have a goal to have a certain amount of money saved by the end of the year for a deposit on a house? Set some goals, prioritise them and then start with the one that excites you the most or that you feel is the most important. Break it down into specific steps that you can outline for yourself and check off along the way.

Next is *Family.* What goals would you like to set for your family life? Do you want to make Friday nights a regular time for your family to go out together for dinner? Or maybe on Sundays for brunch? Is there a particularly thing you want to do with your family such as a vacation at a specific location? If you have decided on a date and time and can organise, book and pay for everything ahead of time, all your family will have to do is turn up and have an awesome time together. Make it a goal then make it happen. Do you want to spend more quality time with your children by setting aside a time when they can absolutely count on you being there for them? Do you want to schedule in a date night, without the kids, once a week or month for just you and your partner—a time that you two can just know is your special time together away from everyone else, when you get a chance to regularly reconnect as human beings and not as parents?

Set some social goals under *Friends*. How often do you want to go out with your friends or a certain friend? Remember, quantity is not so important as quality. If you and your friends have busy lives, you don't have to set an unrealistic goal of getting together once or twice every week. Regular quality time spent together is all you need to keep friendships alive and healthy. Maybe you could set a goal of getting together to catch up with a particular group of friends once a month or bi-weekly. Perhaps you can all meet for dinner or to play pool, or maybe you could go fishing, hiking or simply throw a football around at a park. Perhaps the location and activity are not important to you and will end up being different each time, so long as you are all spending time together. Talk to and agree with your friend or group of friends on a specific time and day to meet and catch up. Setting a regular routine to spend quality time together will help you fit it into your schedule and keep friendships from growing stale. Time spent around like-minded people who share your interests can be extremely rewarding. An hour or two spent speaking with a close friend over lunch once a week, whether it involves simply catching up on life or pouring out your life's challenges and hopes to each other, is never wasted time.

Finally, set goals for your *Physicality* and Health. Do you want to exercise every day? What time of the day are you going to do it? Is it going to be twenty minutes? Is it going to be once every two or three days? Do you want to pick up a new outdoor sport such as mountain biking or kayaking? Would you like to lose or gain a few kilograms by changing your diet? Anything you would like to achieve that has to do with your physical body or health, write it under this column. Set your goals, write them down and schedule them into your agenda.

Making specific goals for yourself like this by writing them down, organising, prioritising and working them into your schedule, is the best way to achieve the things you wish to accomplish. There may be many things you want to do or obtain but if you don't outline your goals in this manner, they may end up falling to the wayside or simply being pushed out of your life by other things that call to your attention. If you don't decide on specific steps and times to follow through with all of your goals, you will find it much harder to make the time required to achieve them. Your dreams will not become reality unless you invest the time and energy necessary in making them reality. Your hopes and desires will never come to fruition unless you have a strategy and this strategy has been proven to work wonders in doing just that—turning one's dreams into reality.

So go through each area of your life and write down your goals in this manner. Don't forget to make them realistic and to set reminders for yourself in your phone or tablet, otherwise either print or write them down and post them somewhere that is clearly visible to you every day.

~ Chapter Twelve ~
VISUALISATION

Visualize this thing that you want, see it, feel it, believe in it. Make your mental blue print, and begin to build. ~ Robert Collier

Seeing is believing and believing that you can achieve something is a crucial ingredient to the formula for success. When you are able to picture in your mind the end of a, sometimes, very long road to achieving a goal, this can help you to truly believe that you can reach that goal. Keeping the end in sight can help give you the determination needed to push through those times when you simply feel like giving up or progress is going slow.

I believe that until you can truly see it, you won't believe it. If you can't picture your success in your own mind then it's unlikely that you are going to believe that it can happen. If you don't feel that you are valuable and that you deserve something, you will not get very far in achieving the kind of success you desire because the universe can only give you what you already believe you have. The process I am about to outline for you will allow you to tap into that sense of self-worth and thus, allow things to happen quicker and more effortlessly for you.

When I go through this process with my own goals, I tap into the seven areas of life and just visualise: I see myself as a spiritual teacher standing in front of an audience helping them to grow and coaching more people on how to be at peace. I see what it's like; I see myself walking onto a stage and I feel what it's like to be there helping and serving people. I close my eyes and I see it in my mind; I feel what it's like. I see the people looking at me. I see the love coming my way and I feel what it's like to be on a bigger stage, sharing my knowledge with a bigger audience than ever before.

Then I move on to the intellectual area of my life and I see myself writing my next book. I see the cover. I see myself being inspired to write it and how it's just pouring out of me; it's not taking a huge effort, the correct words just seem to come. I see myself writing it, getting it out into the world and helping more people through it. I see myself hosting workshops and mentoring others. I visualise myself doing these things; I see it and I can feel it. I can see what it's like to be there standing around watching it happen. I can see the smiles start appearing on people's faces and can sense the peace in the atmosphere. I can sense the shift that is happening in these people as they find a state of calm and balance, and I'm excited by it. I can see it in the room and I can feel it. I feel what it's like to be that person guiding people on that journey.

Then in the area of money and finances, I see myself living in the house that my family has built. I walk in and I can see my children playing happily. I visualise myself walking through the house with my wife, admiring the work we have put into building this home for our family with the money I have been able to make. I also visualise that everything is cheap. If you start to think about what prices will be like in ten years from now, you would realise that everything now is really quite inexpensive. So I visualise everything being cheap and I feel like I've got more money coming in than going out. I visualise myself with money in abundance, like it's on tap; all I need to do to turn that tap on is to serve more people. I visualise all this and I affirm that this is already coming; it's on its way and I am worthy of it.

And then I visualise my family life. I see the quality time I am able to spend with my wife and my kids. I see us playing together and having a great time. I see the house we would love to live in and the travelling we would love to do. I see us sharing the experiences and learning from other cultures and giving back to other people less-fortunate than us.

I also visualise how I want my friendships to be; I feel how I want a special connection with the people close to me. I see it and I plan to make it a reality. I picture some of the places where we will get together regularly. I see us spending quality time together sharing stories and advice and information. I see us really listening to each other and growing together.

Finally, I visualise myself as being physically healthy—having the best-shaped body that I've ever had, having more energy than ever and being able to give to people with that endless supply of energy. I see myself never feeling rundown or burnt out. I see myself loving what I do and that allows me to have the energy to keep going, to keep serving more people.

I have walked you through the process that I use to visualise my goals in order to give you a clear example of how you can do the same. It is a simple process and doesn't require any special techniques nor does it need to take a huge chunk of time out of your day. It doesn't even involve a pen and a paper.

The important thing is that you realise just how powerful this activity can be for you if you stop every once in awhile and take the time to paint those pictures in your mind. It will help keep you on track with your goals and give you the boost of motivation you need to follow through with them. Remember, keep your eye on the light at the end of the tunnel and you will be less tempted to give up when things get rough or progress seems to slow down.

Many of you may know the story about world-famous female Olympic swimmer, Florence Chadwick, who attempted to swim the Catalina Channel at the age of thirty-four on July 4, 1952. Catalina Island is located off the coast of California. Swimming the twenty-one miles from Catalina Island to Palos Verde on the Californian Coast would be the equivalent of completing a full marathon. The day Chadwick set out, the weather was as foul as could be. Thick fog covered the ocean and the choppy water was bitterly cold. The fog was so thick that she could just barely make out the support boats that were following her on either side in case of any emergency. Chadwick swam for hours but finally, after more than 15 hours, she said that she could go no further. She and her crew returned to the shore and were informed that they had been a mere few miles from reaching land at the point where she had given up. Chadwick told reporters that if she had just been able to see the shore, she would have been able to complete the attempt but the fog had been far too thick, making visibility close to impossible and her body had given in.

Just two months later, Chadwick attempted to swim the channel again and this time was successful. She broke a 27-year-old record and became the first woman to ever swim the Catalina Channel.

When news reporters asked her how she had done it, she replied, "I kept the shoreline visualised in my mind the entire time I was swimming."

~ Chapter Thirteen ~

MEDITATION AND TAPPING INTO THE INTUITION

Quiet the mind, and the soul will speak. ~ *Ma Jaya Sati Bhagavati*

Once you have taken the action steps outlined in this book towards discovering inner peace, you will find that you have balanced out all areas of your life and will feel more fulfilled than ever before. You will know the Five Keys to Inner Peace. You will have the tools you need to maintain the balance you have reached. You will also be able to identify which area of your life is out of balance at any given time and bring it back into a balanced state by using these tools.

If you are ever feeling depressed or unwell, it may be because you are down and having negative thoughts about yourself, so read your list and remind yourself about the wonderful things you already have in your life. Ask yourself: *Do I feel this way because somebody said something and I wasn't able to read the subtitles?* If you take a moment to think back on the interaction that caused your negative feelings, you will be able to replay it in your mind; this time reading the subtitles and realising that the situation really had nothing to do with you. Once you go through the steps, you will realise you have placed your emotions back in balance.

If there is a thought that has been sitting in your head too long and keeping you awake at night, you will be able to go through the Five Keys in your mind to find out why this thought is bothering you. Then you can simply observe it and throw it away. If it is repetitive and not serving any good purpose, you can make the conscious decision to not feed it and it will stop coming back to bother you.

You might identify that your feelings of depression or restlessness stem from you failing to be present, so you can make a conscious decision to live only in the moment, right here and now.

Or it might be that you've labelled something as 'good' or 'bad' and this is upsetting you because you are harbouring regret or a grudge against someone else. Now you will know how to balance things out again and reach that state of peace by following the simple action steps you have been given, the tools at your disposal.

The Five Keys are something that you will be able to carry with you for the rest of your life. There will always be times that you become emotionally, mentally, socially or physically off-balance in some manner. However, if you stick to using the Keys, you will always be able to find and reach that balance and place of inner peace once again.

Something that can help you on this journey is meditation. Initially, this may conjure up pictures of yoga mats or cross-legged monks in your mind but there are various forms of meditation and I am going to show you the simplest way I know. I am by no means an expert in this but I want to share with you some techniques that I have learned and use regularly to clear my mind in order to help me find a state of calm from which creativity can flow.

The method I use is based on what Dr Wayne Dyer teaches in his book, *Getting in the Gap*. Once you understand that your brain, by nature, wants to have predictability so it can increase your chances of survival, you can use this strategy to calm yourself by giving it something predictable through the following activity: Sit in a comfortable place free of noise or other people. It is not necessary to have your arms folded or legs crossed. Just sit however you are most comfortable. Next turn your head slowly to one side and look off in that direction as though you were watching something. Imagine you see a tennis player hitting a ball over the net in the middle of a tennis court and on the other side, you see the ball travel over the net slowly. The whole process is playing out in slow motion. Then you turn your head to watch the imaginary tennis ball being hit by the opposing tennis player and it sails back over the net once again. Then the first player hits the ball with his racket and it flies towards the net in slow motion a second time, but this time, the ball falls short and ends up hitting the net. It falls to the ground and sits there motionless. Stop right there and begin to just focus on your breathing for a few moments. Breathe in slowly through your nose if possible. Hold the breath a few moments and then slowly breathe out through your mouth. Relax. Do this a few times until you feel your entire body relax and begin to calm.

Now repeat this process again but with your eyes closed. Just breathe normally and relax your shoulders. If you do this for five or ten minutes every morning, you will notice that you get a clarity that will help you start off every day from a place of calm and focussed energy.

It was from a place of inner peace and calm that my system, The Five Keys to Inner Peace, came to be, which I now teach to high school students and adults across the world. The idea to start motivational speaking and eventually, my tutoring business, all came from this same place of peace and focus. I didn't find peace because I found the system. I discovered the system when I found inner peace. So when people ask me where I 'got all this stuff from' and how I was able to put it into such a simple, direct system, I can honestly say that it was from that place of inner peace and mediation that my greatest ideas came to me.

Does it make sense that when you are in your mind too much and letting an overwhelming volume of thoughts perpetually consume your attention, that the creative part of you, the ultimate source of life, can't come through? It gets clouded, choked out. However, when you are observing your thoughts and calmly letting them float off, you are being present and you have put the ego to sleep in the passenger seat, you will be calm and silent. You will notice that your greatest ideas and creativity will come to you in these times.

I read recently how many companies in Japan are actually building 'silent rooms' into their workplaces where workers can go to take breaks throughout the day and sit in silence for a few moments to meditate so that their creative juices can flow. Apparently, they get some amazing ideas in there because the silence allows that to happen and the owners and managers of these companies have realised this and taken action towards encouraging it. I don't doubt that their businesses are benefitting greatly from this unique and innovative idea.

So don't be afraid of silence. Make regular time for silence. I go away for regular weekends to the mountains on my own to be sure I have enough quiet time and a break from the hectic life I live. I switch off my phone and I just read or I write. I go for a hike and just spend time in nature on my own. I find that ideas, that want to come through to me, always come through at those time when I've stilled my mind and allowed myself some space from the usual rush and business of life.

Apart from the meditation, there is one other thing I suggest you do.

Are there some big questions you have been asking yourself or searching desperately for the answers to? Take any question that you want—it could have to do with spirituality, for example. It might be that you want to feel closer to God. Ask yourself what it is that you need to do in order to make this happen and just sit in silence for several moments. Don't try and think of the answer but rather, let the answer come to you. Just sit there and be patient. It might not come to you right away or even today but if you just repeat the process, it will come.

Same too with intellectuality. You may be asking yourself: *What is it that I really want to read into or research? What am I passionate about and want to learn more about?* Just sit there in silence and allow the answers to come to you. Don't force them; just allow them to come to you and they will.

When it comes to work or vocation, your question may be: *What is the greatest service I can provide to humanity on this planet?* Again, just sit there and wait for the answer to come. You might also ask yourself: *If money was no issue and nobody's opinion mattered, what would I do for fun and get paid to do?* Keep a notepad next to you and write down anything that comes to you.

Perhaps you have a question to ask about your family life. It may be: *What can I do to make my relationship with my partner stronger?* Or: *How do I reconnect with my children?* If you are in a place of inner peace, you will find that natural connections start to happen, that you may decide you want to make a conscious decision to set aside a certain amount of time on a particular day each week to regularly spend time with them. So as you can see, the answers and inspiration will really just come to you if you are patient and at peace.

When it comes to friendship, ask yourself any question you'd like answered. Just sit there and wait for the answer to come to you. It may be: *Do I really need this many friends in my life?* Or maybe, *How do I get closer to my best friends? How can I connect with them better?* Just wait for the answers to come to you.

Finally, ask yourself what you need to do to be healthier and happier. Just sit there and allow the answer to come to you. Don't let it come from your mind. Just notice where your answers are coming from in this process in all areas of your life. You don't want your answer to come from your mind, which would be from the ego. In this case, the ego might say: *Go train really hard. Spend two hours in the gym six days a week so you look really good and people notice you.* However, the intuition might tell you: *Just walk, twenty or thirty minutes a day. Do some swimming. Do something you enjoy. Do something that's low-impact but that does a lot for your health. Don't overdo it. Choose an activity that you can sustain day by day and have the motivation to continue so that you can keep exercising regularly, which will benefit your health much more in the long run.*

Now you have learned the Five Keys to Inner Peace as well as some further advice on ways you can get yourself motivated, inspired and productive. However, this is not the end of your journey. Knowing is one thing. You must also be motivated and committed to the actions towards reaching that place from which abundance, inspiration and creativity can flow endlessly. Anyone can do it. It has worked for hundreds already and will work for you too, as long as you are willing to follow the steps.

The tasks are not difficult; they do not pull you way out of your comfort zone. They will simply require that you make certain changes in the way you see and interact with the world around you. With time and practice, the behaviours in this book will become second nature for you and you will be able to maintain that state of balanced peace and calm for the rest of your life.

The abundance that flows into your life from your newfound inner peace will overflow into the lives of those around you; you will become a walking, breathing example for many. You will begin to touch and change the world and make a bigger difference than you ever thought possible.

So let the peace in and the drama out and watch how you transform into a truly invincible soul—a being capable of changing the world.

THE MEANING OF LOVE

And still, after all this time, the Sun has never said to the Earth, "You owe me."
Look what happens with love like that. It lights up the sky. ~ Rumi

People sometimes ask me the question, "What is love?"

To me, love is being able to see the positives and the negatives in someone (including yourself) at the same time and realise that we need both sides of the coin. Love is neither dismissing nor putting down the Shadow Side but embracing it as part of the whole and realising the beauty to the balance.

I used to think that I wanted both my parents to be like my mother. My mother was always doing everything for me and was very protective, whereas my father was once very critical, judgemental and I often felt that he was putting me down. However, I now realise that I've always needed them just the way they are. If both my parents were like my mother, I'd still be juvenile and dependent. I know that I wouldn't have left home by now. I'd be having trouble with relationships, with finding work and with furthering my life in general because I'd be expecting everybody to do everything for me. As for my father's perfectionism—I realise now that he wasn't happy with his own life at one point so he found ways to take out his frustration on me. That helped me to be able to become an independent person. It made me stop and take a look within myself. The pain that I felt from how he treated me, brought me closer to spiritual awakening. I am very grateful today. I realise that I needed the balance between the challenge and support I got from my parents to become the person I am today.

You will find that in many families, there is that balance. There seems to be one parent playing the 'good cop' and other one playing the 'bad cop'.

Now, ideal parenting is when both parents can give love and support in equal amounts. When a child feels that you love them, meaning that you support them and challenge them, you can explain things to them in a calm way. You can tell them that you love them and this is why you are doing what you are doing for their own good. When you are able to explain things to them in a calm manner, they feel loved; they don't feel threatened. The ego backs down, goes to sleep and the child can actually listen to what you are saying.

If you think about the greatest professor you've ever had or your favourite sports coach or music teacher, it's usually the one who gave you both support and challenge in equal amounts that sticks in your memory and really helped you grow.

For example, if you had a coach who was always 'buddy-buddy' with you, cracking jokes all through practice and making fun but didn't challenge you, you might enjoy your time spent with him but you probably wouldn't grow to reach your full potential. Alternatively, you could have a coach who was constantly screaming, yelling and never happy with what you were doing; perhaps you would get some results but probably not the best results that you could get because his method would wear thin on you and you wouldn't enjoy it.

In contrast, when you have a coach who gives you equal love and support while also challenging you, you realise that you grow the most. They are the ones who push you to a higher level and you know that they love and care about you, that it's not just about the results for them but it's about helping you grow as a person.

In the sporting field recently, there has been a greater emphasis on people management. There are many coaches who know their sport, know what it takes to win, but aren't adept at managing human beings, at giving them equal love and support with challenge. Some are just too challenging without the love and that wears thin on players, and generally, those coaches eventually find themselves without a job.

Then there are coaches who just try and be the players' best mates and get along all the time so that they are liked. In the end, this doesn't get much better results and they too find themselves out of a job.

Ultimately, you will find that the greatest managers in the world, whether it be in the sporting field, in business or simply in one's household, are the ones who give love in terms of equal support and challenge to their employees, to their players or their families whom they are guiding.

To become an effective leader in your life, whether it means being a good parent or a role model for your colleagues at work, you must be able to strike the balance between giving love in equal amounts of challenge and support. When you can bring both of these together in equal parts, people will listen to you and they will respect you. They will realise that you want them to grow and that you truly care about them as human beings. You will also be able to articulate this rather than just being an authoritarian who only gives challenge, or trying to be their best mate, being too soft and allowing people to walk all over you.

As always, you realise that the balance must be struck, that neither one is good nor bad, that you really do need both. You cannot be one-side and if you are trying to be, that's where your frustration will come from.

I coach a lot of people who complain to me that they often feel they are being taken advantage of. I simply show them that nothing in your life happens without your permission. If you are being too nice, it's because you don't value yourself enough and are desperately seeking external validation: *I need to get everybody to value me; I have to be a people-pleaser. I need people to like me so I have to be super nice to them all, even if that means letting them walk all over me.* And then there are people who complain that some people just don't do what they say, that they're just being difficult. So I explain to them how both children and adults are much more responsive to your wishes when they know that you love them and care about them. So if you want to challenge them, that's fine, but you need to give them some support also. You need to get them to see that you are only wanting to give them equal amounts of support and challenge so that they can grow, then you will find that the people you work with and the people around you at home will just be able to accept things much easier, and you will be able to become a leader. You will be able to help them grow to their maximum and reach their full potential.

To become the best leader that you can be, it really comes down to the extent to which you've owned all the traits. It comes down to being able to accept that we all have two sides to us, just as our sets of values are two-sided coins and cannot be separated. It comes down to being able to find that balance and from there, you will find and emanate peace.

Dr Demartini went through an English dictionary from cover to cover and found there are 4,628 words that are used to describe traits in the English language, and yes, he went through all of them. Every time he came to a trait, he thought of a person that most embodied that particular trait. He then went through the Demartini process and owned up to the trait himself and then went on to own up the opposite side. He did this with all the positive traits and all the negative ones.

I'm not saying you should grab the next English dictionary you can find and take a week off work to own up to every trait within its covers. The point is that the concept of this process is all about quitting a nasty habit of placing people up on pedestals above you or pushing them below you by rating their characteristics, labelling them as 'bad' or 'good'. The people whom you rate below you, you resent. Anybody you place above you, you are infatuated with. Neither is love. By going through this process, you learn to love yourself, which then allows you to love other people. You will no longer look up to people and see them as better than you or more special than you because you will see that there's nothing in them that's not within you; you just haven't allowed it to come out; you just haven't given yourself permission to let it shine.

This is something that I continue to do in my life. I've taken the greatest philosophers, the greatest minds, the greatest teachers in the world and I'm in the process of looking at their traits, their characteristics, their teachings and owning them; realising that there's nothing within them that's not within me. I also let myself see the negatives, to realise that they're not perfect people but their negatives serve a purpose. There's nothing wrong with the way they are; they're just human beings. Both the positives and negatives must come together as one to foster people to grow to their highest potential.

And that is love.

Coaching Progress Report

Please score yourself from 0-10 for each area. 0 strongly disagree up to 10 for strongly agree

Key	Week 1	Week 2	Week 3	Week 4	Week 5	Week 6	Week 7	Week 8
# 1 Learn to Love Yourself I love and accept myself unconditionally								
# 2 Read the Subtitles I can look beyond the words of what people say and not let them affect me								
# 3 Be Aware of Your Thoughts I only allow negative thoughts to stay in my mind for a very brief time								
# 4 Be Present I am conscious of being present for the majority of my day								
# 5 There is No Good or Bad I see the divine order in life and no longer label events, traits in myself or other people as bad								

Printed in the United States
By Bookmasters